C000082618

SILE

AND THE DISORDER OF

TONGUES

SILENCE

AND THE DISORDER OF TONGUES

ERIC RHODE

APEX ONE

First published in 2016 by Apex One
7 Hillsleigh Road
London W8 7LE

British Library Cataloguing in
Publication Data

A C.I.P. for this book is available from
the British Library

ISBN: 978-0-9935100-4-5

Edited by Communication Crafts

Designed by Bradbury & Williams

Printed by CMP (UK) Ltd

Books by the same author

Tower of Babel

*A History of the Cinema from Its
Origins to 1970*

On Birth & Madness

The Generations of Adam

Psychotic Metaphysics

*On Intuition, Hallucination and the
Becoming of "O"*

Plato's Silence

Notes on the Aniconic

Axis Mundi

On Revelation

It is my wish to leave everything that I can think of and choose for my love the thing that I cannot think.

[ANON., *THE CLOUD OF UNKNOWING*, IN GRIFFIN, 1981: 20]

Silence is a symbol of the future world.
[ISAAC OF NINEVEH, IN WENSINCK, 1923: 315]

How I conceive of silence is how I conceive of mind. And how I conceive of mind enables me, or disables me, in the process of recognising how and why silence should be so meaningful. My concern is one that does not involve explanation. It does not involve the type of understanding in which explanation is helpful. But habit being what it is, I shall have difficulty in resisting the impulse to explain. Silence is a potency beyond measure. It is beyond understanding. Or rather it is irrelevant to understanding, which follows its own very interesting paths. Recognising the potency of silence depends on the extent to which mind is able to recognise its own ground in the unknowable. I cannot separate silence and the unknowable. If I open myself to silence, I find that an intuition of the unknowable has gained access to me. In acts of contemplation I think of silence as approaching and entering me, but I cannot know its source, and this not knowing is a presence. It feels to be other than myself. There is the sense of a limitless depth without an object to locate the depth.

In Plato's *Timaeus* a demiurge generates time and the movement of the heavens out of eternity. Time and the movement of the heavens, like silence, approach and enter me; but eternity is a form of the unknowable, and I have no understanding of how the unknowable can be the motive for knowledge. The demiurge personifies the intelligence of any thinking being: god-like in appearance, he brings about transformation in a breath-taking way, even though his supernatural powers are limited. "He determined to make a moving image of eternity, and so when he ordered the heavens he made in that which we call time an eternal moving image of the eternity which remains for ever at one" (Plato, *Timaeus* 37, in Lee, 1965: 51). There is no way to account for this act. If I attempt to explain it, I find that I lapse into the demotic of magic. Plato presents the transformation as a cosmological fact. I cannot accept this, but I do I find its poetry meaningful as an intuition about the nature of mind. For the concept of eternity, I would stipulate the existence of an unknowable ground to mind, the immeasurable, which exists in a generative alliance with the possibility of measure and with the generation of mind itself. I propose that without this unfathomable potency there would be no mind. It is the closest I can come to understanding the idea that mind might have a ground. In this respect mind is unlike the brain.

The age-old distinction between an active life and a contemplative life can present itself as a distinction between two different ways of living a life. Only at a remove does this distinction present itself as being about ways of imagining mind's relation to silence. In the active life, mind is able to gain a focus on almost everything, apart from silence. It is purposive in its acts of administration. It is instrumental. It is not distracted or delayed. It sees itself as a subject in relation to an object, which is the world, and the world presses in on it, insisting on fulfilment. Silence when glimpsed is an irritant, an embarrassment, and sometimes oppressive. It is the awkward pause in a conversation, or the phantom of night in a countryside in which the distant barking of a dog is a relief. Townsfolk who feel at ease with the active life flee from this silence at first light. In effect, silence in the active life presents itself as a premonition of death. Again I might say: the silence of the dead victim haunts the murderer.

In the active life, time and space give no place to the immeasurable. They are measures used to resist the poetry of transformation. They are like the glass of the windowpane against which a fly beats as it attempts to reach the light. I cannot penetrate the transparent glass, I cannot release myself from the strictures of time and space; and yet I glimpse something beyond. I want to move out of the life of action. I want to relate measure to a means of deliverance by way of a Platonic kind of demiurge, but I cannot. I have the wrong set of mind.

Everything changes when I move from the active life to the contemplative life. I move from an exercise of reason and understanding to a state in which I think to bear witness to the inexplicable. I no longer discredit silence. It is at the centre; it wells up within and without me. The more I open myself to silence, the more its generosity is abundant. And I realise that it is the closest that I can come to the immeasurable in conscious experience.

I now see the glass of the windowpane from a different perspective. Time and space assume a different aspect. They no longer constrain insight: as vehicles to the unknowable, they are radiant with its light. In contemplation mind opens itself to itself without any need for explanation. It is in harmony with a fundamental alliance between the measurable and the immeasurable. The radiance of Plato's time is the radiance of an alliance between the measurable (time) and the immeasurable (eternity). This is how mind is when it sets aside the rigours that enable it to survive in the active life. A capacity for wonder overrides the claims of reason. It lays claim to a progression that is uniquely a symbolism of wonder. Fundamental to this transformation is silence.

The infinite abyss of contemplation.
[GREGORY OF NYSSA, IN DANIÉLOU, 1962: 88]

I find myself travelling at speed above the ocean and in a night that is total in its darkness. A vast, encircling and yet narrow rim of light emerges all around beneath me. If I experience the darkness as natural, I shall expect the trace of light in darkness to yield itself up to explanation, which so happens as night disappears with the coming of dawn, and the rim of light shows itself to be the horizon. But let me think of the darkness imaginatively, as a metaphysical darkness that is without direction and that cannot be explained. Let me think further that it is inseparably part of the metaphysic on which psychology is grounded. Any trace of light that might appear is mysterious because it cannot be explained. This is how a symbol appears. In wonder a symbol realises itself. Without wonder there is no symbol. It is always a first beginning, like the spirit that unfolds far within a creation narrative. Plato's demiurge in this state of the within must have known disorientation in creating time out of eternity. He sought for time as a foothold in the void.

Bertrand Russell in *The ABC of Relativity* has a verbal diagram explain a principle in Einstein's physics. The poetry in the description, which is implicit rather than stated, enables me to see it as a symbol in the making. The symbol comes from nowhere; it might have its source in dream or in a moment of vision. In terms of explanation, the balloon comes from nowhere, and where it is going nobody knows.

> Suppose that on a dark night a number of men with lanterns were walking in various directions across a huge plain, and suppose that on one part of the plain there was a hill with a flaring beacon in the top. Our hill is to be such as we have described, growing steeper as it goes up and ending in a precipice. I shall suppose that there are villages dotted about the plain and the men with lanterns are walking to and from the various villages. Paths have been made showing the easiest way from any one village to any other. These paths will be more or less curved, to avoid going up the hill; they will be more sharply curved when they pass near the top of the hill than when they keep some way off it. Now suppose you are observing all of this, as best you can, from a place high up in a balloon, so that you cannot see the ground, but only lanterns and the beacon. You will not know that there is a hill, or that the beacon is at the top of it.

You will see the people turn out of the straight course when they approach the beacon, and that the nearer they come the more they turn aside. You will naturally attribute this to an effect of the beacon; you may think it is it is exerting some force on the lantern. But if you wait for daylight you will find that the beacon merely marks the top of the hill and does not influence the people with lanterns in any way. . . . Now in this analogy the beacon corresponds to the sun, the people with lanterns correspond to the planets and the comets, the paths correspond to their orbits, and the coming of daylight corresponds to the coming of Einstein.

[RUSSELL, 1925: 79–80]

The traveller in the balloon is aware of an irregular dance of lights. He cannot explain to himself what the traces of light might mean. Russell says nothing about the condition of the traveller. The balloon drifts through darkness. There is no indication that the traveller has a compass. Russell offers two explanations for what the traveller sees. One is in terms of the people who move with flares up and around an imperceptible hill, and the other is in terms of Einstein's non-naturalistic explanation of the unpredictable light movements. But let me imagine this situation differently, as one without an explanation. There is an alliance in mind between measure and the immeasurable that generates mind. Between the parts of the alliance there is an unknowable potential in which measure, if it exists, is unstable. Out of an alliance, in which the immeasurable is the unknowable, there comes into being silence as well as measure.

Russell's balloon drifts as though through nowhere. There is no point of reference inside or outside. In fact, there is no cosmos, only the formless infinite. There is no explanation. In another context, Russell discusses the idea of place. "The whole notion that one is always in some definite place is due to the fortunate immobility of most of the large objects on the earth's surface. The idea of 'place' is a rough practical approximation: there is nothing logically necessary about it, and it cannot be made precise" (Russell, 1925: 12). The traveller in the balloon is without a sense of the located. And yet his condition potentially is one of revelation. The movement of the distant lights creates an iconography that is sufficient unto itself. It is analogous to what I imagine to be a foetal dawning of consciousness. And this is how the cosmos might originate in a creationist narrative.[1]

The balloon's journey through darkness is redolent of the nineteenth century: it has a patrician feeling to it; it looks down on a world that does not yield up the secret of its reality. It finds its touchstone in the act of verifying fact, whether scientific or historical: a procedure that can lead to misunderstanding when the subject is the inexplicable, as Wittgenstein pointed out with some vehemence in regard to Frazer's contempt for tribal peoples who had no knowledge of physics (Wittgenstein, 1967). It is as though, in spite of any inten-

[1] And yet the claim to any beginning in creation narrative must be called in doubt. Creation narratives, for all their claim to sequence, are cyclical. They are narratives of renewal or eternal return. The concept of beginning with its sense of uniqueness belongs elsewhere. The darkness and the light of creation narrative are in their potency dreadful beyond understanding, and only the repetition of rite and ceremony can seem to assuage this power.

tion, Russell had produced a remarkable symbol for awe. His diagram describes an occurrence that is without touchstone. If it is a revelation, it is not an event. In fact, a revelation is a catastrophe that disrupts the order of time and space and cannot be compared to an event. In my understanding, the journey through darkness has a religious significance. It signifies the meaning of being the one who is sacrificed. "When the sixth hour came, darkness fell over the whole land until the ninth hour" (Mark 15: 33). Out of this womb of death, which I call the transfiguring womb of the father, emerges a symbol that (as it were) puts the demiurgic time and space transformation of the *Timaeus* into reverse.

In Russell's balloon I travel through a darkness that is without limit. The traces of light that I meet with are incomprehensible. My perception of irregularity reflects the uncertainty of my experience of movement in darkness. I have no means of orientation; I am in the father's womb. Any link between movement and direction is broken. The thought occurs to me that I am in touch with the unfolding of a principle that is formative in creationist narrative. Conceivably, this is how the demiurge understands sensation in his attempt to extract time and the heavens out of eternity. This is how it must be to find oneself lost within the generative alliance of the measurable and the immeasurable.

I understand the experience of being in Russell's balloon as a case of being at a point of transition between the immeasurable and the measurable or the unknowable and the knowable. This is how it would feel to be at such a point. There would be little or no clue as to the meaning of the transition. The ritual of the sacrifice is a ritual of division within the awe of an unknowable experienced as silence that enacts the meaning of this point of transition. At this point – which clearly is an inexact way of describing the transition – Plato's demiurge enables time and space to emerge from the immeasurable, or enables it to return into the immeasurable.

Long after I had completed this book, I came to realise that what I think of as my father's unconscious projection into me of the horrors of trench warfare in the First World War (about which for the most part he was silent) informs my fascination with the darkness that surrounds Russell's balloon. The aura of the father's womb in this case appears to be a way of describing an unconscious projection from father into son.

It is by awakening to the feeling of being a stranger that the soul of the Gnostic discovers where it is. At the same time it has a sense of foreboding concerning where it has come from and to where it might be returning.
[HENRY CORBIN, 1954: 19]

The truths of contemplation depend on a capacity to be receptive. The more open the mind is, the more is it capable of depth. The nature of the sexual undercurrent to this receptivity is unique. In the narrative of the Annunciation, a young woman is reading a book. She is receptive to the text. The Holy Spirit appears to her in the form of an angel, and from the breath of the Holy Spirit her womb receives a unique life. In Buddhist terms, she receives the seed of enlightenment. In Christian terms, she receives the Word, and the Word she receives is inseparable from the meaning of the sacrifice. Within the receptivity of her silence is a plenitude that the imagination cannot realise. The one who practises contemplation enters into modes of apprehension that are inaccessible to the active life. The self that lives the active life is unable to see why the silence of contemplation might be a wellspring to insight. And yet the two lives are not that distant. On the borderline between them, images of the active life are drawn into the life of contemplation. Russell's balloon and Plato's demiurge are representations that reflect on an abyss that is inherent in the act of contemplation.

Vedic thinkers conceive of silence rather than the Word as the body of the sacrifice. In contradistinction, Christian thinkers conceive of the Word rather than silence as the sacrifice. Silence and the Word are unlike and yet inseparable in the imagination. When together, they are the sacrifice; they arouse the grief and the disorder of tongues, which lies within the generative alliance of the measurable and the immeasurable. It is conceivable that foetal consciousness at its point of origination might exist within this atmosphere of disjunction and hope. In acts of contemplation, silence and the sacrifice are like the roots to a tree that in its growing shows itself to be a symbol that requires neither time nor space in order to establish itself.

In Vedic thought, the severing of the god Prajâpati is the sacrifice. Silence and the body of Prajâpati are as one; the silence is the sacrifice. The impulse that shows forth creation as the symbol of life lies in this identification.

> According to the Brāhmana, words and other means of expression (*nirukta*) co-exist with the inexpressible (*anirukta*) as the undefined, the unlimited and the uncertain. Anirukta signifies among other meanings length of life, the future, breath and thought (*manas*).

Silence gives expression to thought. As a certain text says: breath devours the word of the one who is silent. Another text states that a priest who spreads out the skin of an antelope affirms by this act that the skin is the sacrifice. The sacrifice is Prajâpati, and Prajâpati is the inexpressible.

[RENOU, 1949: 15] [1]

Louis Renou describes ritual silence as having singular virtues; it is the root to the sacrifice as well as its eye (tree roots are associated to silence because voices, however close, are unable to reach them). The meaning of the sacrifice is evident in ritual silence. It is lost in the practice of speech. To follow speech with a silent oblation avoids any movement from the same to the same. It draws attention to the values of engenderment. It averts discord among the gods. It avoids any contamination by the perishable and the discriminated. Silence reaches out to the inexpressible and surmounts the total and the unbounded; it surmounts even the world of the

[1] Prajâpati is akin to all silence. He concentrates in his person all that passes beyond the limited and sensible. He represents the brahman (neuter), the old symbol of the enigma charged with silence that has an exceptional place in the bramodya or exchange of enigmas (riddles). The brahman (neuter) is inexpressible, and it is not by chance that the brahman (masculine), or bearer of the brahman, is to be found in the silent official who presides over the Vedic sacrifice (Renou, 1949).
    'Opening the mind to silence marks a transition from the measurable into the immeasurable. Silence at this point of transition is associated with acts of sacrifice. On the level of concrete thought, Plato's demiurge responds to the immeasurable as though it were a body that could be divided in such a way that it shows itself to be the measures of time and space. Prajâpati is my basic model for understanding the sacrifice. But twice-sacrificed Osiris, who is known as the lord of silence in ancient Egyptian belief, is another model, and so is the Christ whose body in the ceremony of the Eucharist is divided among the worshippers. For Christ's relation to silence see J. N. M. Wijngaards: "Jesus' silence is a datum of ancient tradition firmly embedded in the passion accounts" ' (Wijngaards, 1975).

gods. It excludes any adversary. . . . Moreover, it is relevant for acts of expiation, and for funeral rites; and it sets in motion forces that are without definition (paraphrase of Renou, 1949: 14).

Silence is the primal moment. It enters the Word by way of the vowel OM, out of which everything stems. The cosmos takes on being out of this one sound. This is how silence might speak if it were to speak. The tongue plays no part in this rite. OM is more an articulated breath than a means to eloquence. In a spectral way, it points to the enunciated; it marks the first stirrings of renewal; it is in its rising up, and in a virtual way, the first cosmic axial.

If Vedic silence enacts the inexplicable or enigmatic nature of the sacrifice, then the Vedic Word is evidence of a tenseless being. "The phonemes that compose the Veda are by nature eternal and they endorse the claims of the Veda to be eternal. *Shabda* signifies both 'sound' and 'word'. It is comparable to space. Its potency is without limit. . . . Sound as eternal relates to sound as experience in the same way as being is related to its realisation: it is one and it cannot be modified" (Renou & Filliozat, 1953: 12). "The Vedic word is uncreated: while it has been the subject of many kinds of revelation, and has forms both concentrated and expanded, it has never had in and of itself a beginning. The primary way of thinking about the Absolute in India is to perceive it as the quintessence of the Vedic word: and this is the primary sense of the word *brahman*" (Malamoud, 1989: 224).

In Vedic thought the sacrifice is inseparable from a silence that the god Prajâpati embodies. The inseparabili-

20

ty is evidence of the unknowable. It is without explanation. The Vedic Word is not directly the act of sacrifice. In the Christianity of the Eastern Church, the Word – as the Son – is the sacrifice. "And when he had opened the seventh seal, then was silence in heaven about the space of half an hour" (Revelations 8: 1 – in contradistinction to Mark 15: 33). Silence is revelation. It draws all antonyms and oxymorons into itself. It draws the sacrifice into itself and then releases it from within itself. The death and resurrection of the Son is analogous to the Vedic sacrifice. Silence is other, and yet it is intimate, and so much within each of us, that it replaces any claim to selfhood. It is the Holy Spirit; it is that which renews and restores; it is the tradition that reforms itself as the new. In relation to the Word it is a working relationship, at one with it while set apart from it, as when out of the heavens the Paracelete appears in tongues of fire that enable the disciples (and the Mother of the Word who is among them) to speak in many languages. The unknowable is the abiding and yet hidden Father who begets the Word as his Son and who by the mysterious theological doctrine of procession enables the grace of the Holy Spirit. Word and silence may conjoin, but their relation to each other is established by their different ways of interceding with the unknowable.

The relation of silence and the sacrifice is apparent at the eleventh hour, in ceremonies at the Cenotaph.

The world was one lip.
[GENESIS 11: 1, WYCLIFFE BIBLE]

[Tradition] is the living breath that makes the word heard at the same time as the silence from which it came.
[LOSSKY, 1959: 151]

In the active life, "it is what it is" means no more and no less than what it says. It is that and no more. The active life must deny itself the spatiality in which a symbol comes into being. It does not allow itself enquiry into the principle that originates intuition. It is without that sort of dimension. On the other hand, in the contemplative life "it is what it is" is the voice in the fire that describes itself as "I am that I am". The fire is as elliptical as the voice that speaks from within it. It is non-processual and without combustion; it has no need to feed on anything.

The difference between the active and the contemplative life appears unbridgeable; and yet if silence enters representations of the actual, it can have the representations assume a contemplative significance. I had an experience of this kind in the Boijmans Van Beuningen Museum in Rotterdam. I was looking at one of the four representations of the Tower of Babel by Pieter Bruegel the elder. (It is known as the small Tower of Babel, to distinguish it from his Tower of Babel in the Kunsthistorisches Museum in Vienna.) While looking at it, I began to associate the painting to silence. The painting appeared to emanate silence. It was as though silence were a radiance arising from within it. The relation between the painting and silence was insistent, although I could discover no conscious link between them. At the time I was far from understanding how silence, in its aesthetic aspect and in relation to an artefact, might be generative of meanings of a specific kind.

With the passing of time, long after I had left Rotterdam, I came to think of the painting itself, and the tower that it depicted, as armatures by means of which silence radiates. The notion of armature was crucial to understanding the way in which the artist and the spectator communicate. In one respect silence is deep in its stillness. In another respect its speed is faster than any sound. The artist in the act of painting enters a contemplative silence that, by way of silence, is able to communicate with the contemplative state of the spectator. The shared object, which in this case is a painting, carries a transmission between the artist and the spectator. Silence is the key to aesthetic apprehension. It can be intuited without being recognised. Bruegel's painting is a telling example of the silence that typifies any art of stature; it is a commentary on all great painting, as well as being a great painting itself.

Socrates, in the Phaedrus (275d), refers to "The majestic silence of painting". The greater the painting, the more pervasive is the significance of its silence. Silence enters the visual as though in a solemn and improbable marriage, and in doing so it informs aesthetic greatness.

Silence in the Bruegel generates the contradictions inherent in the painting: this is how silence as an aesthetic operates. One contradiction concerns the difference between the active and the contemplative life. Bruegel's painting reflects the mercantile spirit of the Renaissance. It is about the active life; it is a secular conception of the text from which it is taken, Genesis 11. And yet it is not quite of this world. It is fascinating because it is a symbol of the unknowable. A number of commentators have thought its construction to be as an act of defiance against God, and some of them have assumed that God sought to destroy it. (Genesis 11 says that God confounds the language of the people; it says nothing about God destroying the tower. The idea of destroying the tower derives from later commentators.) The painting is equivocal about destruction. The evidence of destruction is slight and open to doubt. High on the walls of the tower there is an extended transparent reddish tint that might be a residual bloodstain. The incomplete jagged upper level might – or might not – refer to the fact that the building is unfinished, or it might be a premonition concerning a future act of destruction. Whatever the future might hold, the atmosphere among the artisans is one of quiet industry. The atmosphere is calm, even distanced. Numerous small figures work on the terraces: it has been calculated that there are more than a thousand figures on the facing side of the tower alone. The sense of unperturbed industry would appear to reflect the artist's own care for detail. This is how the active life might perceive itself within the mirror of contemplation. This is how the artist himself might have thought about his work in progress.

The architecture of the tower is both practical and unworldly. There is a touch of the fabulous about the way that it lists at an angle to the rectangular shape of the canvas. It might be about to rise up in the air, taking with it a piece of land on which it is built. At the top it appears to extend beneath the frame (or perhaps at one time the canvas was cut back). The vantage point of the spectator, which is parallel to the ramp on the third floor, enables the immense structure to be taken in at one glance. At the same time, the vantage point is disquieting (why, the spectator might ask, am I so high up?) The curved contour of the building lies like a fragile shell against a dark background of identical shape. The tracery of many windows intimates a skull-like presence. The two shapes, of contour and dark background, create a form in being placed together. In general the differentiation of two–dimensional and three-dimensional shape is unclear. Foreground and background are destabilised in relation to each other.

"An object fashioned by the industry of man acquires its reality only in so far as it participates in a transcendental reality" (Eliade, 1949: 5). Bruegel's reverie transforms a perception of how people build a tower into an image that exists within the ideal. Like the forms that Leonardo in reverie discovered in stains on a wall, it is an image discovered among the leaping flames of the burning bush or in the movement of clouds. An aesthetic generated by silence presents itself by way of problems that cannot be solved and by way of questions that cannot be answered. Ambiguities and contradictions cannot be reconciled. Silence presents itself as unbounded by notions of time and space; and by a kind of telepathy it communicates itself everywhere to anyone. Silence is intimate and personal. At the same time, it is a universal transmission like the sunbeam of the Holy Spirit, which "falls on him who enjoys it as though it were for him alone; yet it illuminates land and sea and mingles with the air" (St Basil, *De Spiritu Sancto*, Chapter 9, in Lossky, 1944: 166). The process that communicates silence, clearly silent itself, recalls the snow in Coleridge's notebooks that "on a calm day falling scarce seems to fall & plays & dances in & out, to the very moment that it reaches the ground" (in Coburn, 1961: 228).

Knowing the Truth in the Light which belongs to it and not
according to the natural light of human reason.
[LOSSKY, 1959: 152]

Genesis 11: 1–9 is startling because of its abrupt juxtaposi-
tions. Without explanation, it places side by side the idea of
building the tower with the idea of a single universal language.
"The whole earth", it says, "was one language and one speech."
And then without pause it describes the journey from the east
to a plain in the land of Shinar, where the travellers intend
to build a city as well as a tower "whose top may reach unto
heaven. . . ."

"Let us make a name lest we be scattered abroad upon
the face of the whole earth." The divine presence observes
that "Behold the people is one, and they all have one language
. . . and now nothing will be restrained from them, which they
have imagined to do. . . . Let us go down and there confound

their language, that they may not understand one another's speech." In Genesis it is the city rather than the tower that is called Babel "because the Lord did there confound the language of all the earth; and from thence did the Lord scatter them abroad upon the face of the earth."

In what way is the idea of a universal language related to the people who reach the plain of Shinar and to no one else? Are there no other language-users in the neighbourhood? And why should the multiplication of tongues be thought to be a curse?[1] There are no certain answers. It is relevant to the meaning of language that the tower is built of brick rather than stone. "And they said to one another, Go to, let us make brick and burn them thoroughly. And they had brick for stone and they had slime for mortar." Children who are in the process of learning to speak may be seen vigorously to knock down toy brick structures made by others. They may – or may not – resent the capacity of others to do what they cannot do, which is to speak and to put words together as though they were bricks. Vedic belief equates the bricks out of which the fire altar is built and the words of sacred text. The five levels of the altar are stanzas in a poem, on which as units the existence of moments, hours, days and years depends.[2]

---

[1] Indeed, J. P. Harland has argued on the basis that God wants his people to be fruitful and multiply that the dissemination of languages was intended as an encouragement to the people of the tower since it shook them out of "a fortress mentality that seeks to survive by its own resources" (1998: 528).

[2] "The altar [is] a symbol and the confirmation of an act of genesis. The central and essential event of the genesis is the construction of a time that is possessed of divisions, of a succession of discrete units capable of being grouped into regular sequences. This is the occasion for deep reflection on the part of the Vedic theologians upon the continuous and the discontinuous" (Malamoud, 1989: 215).

They are also the dismembered parts of Prajâpati. Through the integration and disintegration of his body, Prajâpati unites the idea of silence and the sacrifice. The aesthetics of silence becomes silence in its religious aspect, and the silence of the Holy Spirit aligns itself with the sacrifice of Christ. Everything undergoes change in this understanding, and the meaning of the disorder of tongues is plain. A golden figure that represents Prajâpati is buried in the brick altar. It gives rise to meaning in much the same way as the passage of OM through the abdomen and out of the mouth gives meaning to language through silence. An image forms of the cosmic axial within the body. In the Hindu temple, an idol in the darkness of the innermost shine represents the god. It is hidden rather than buried. Its silence animates the bricks of the temple walls and the statues attached to the walls. There is a theophany. The stones that make up the building are as translucent as means of revelation as the skin of the breast can be in the unconscious phantasy life of the one who feeds from it.

The need to question closely the assertions of Genesis 11 is incidental to the effect that it has on the imagination of the spectator drawn to it by its enigmatic nature. I recall a discussion with Donald Meltzer concerning a sculpture whose iconography was reminiscent of Bruegel's tower. It was a bronze semi-sphere that resembled a sliced-open pomegranate, with a flat surface of what looked like seed shapes within it. Donald Meltzer suggested that the sculpture as I described it evoked, in terms of the inner world, a phantasy that a baby at the breast might have concerning seeds within the breast. He alluded to a lecture by Wilfred Bion (or was it a discussion?)

concerning a patient's dream/experience of a moving milk float, out of the back of which fell a crate of glass milk bottles. Some of the bottles were broken by the fall (and presumably some of the milk spilt). In catastrophe (the breaking of the milk bottles) the seed shapes in the pomegranate sculpture might come to resemble the sharp tooth-like shapes of the broken glass. These sharp seed shapes are like the first Thebans who sprang out of the dragon teeth that Jason had sown in the ground. There appears to be a relation between the seeds of procreation that an infant in phantasy might ascribe to the breast and the seeds in its mouth, which are sounds and other verbal potentials that can break down in acts of screaming. What the infant in the adult perceives in the breast reflects the existence of preconceptions concerning the units of language. The equation of seeds, words and broken milk bottles is a case of a disorder of tongues, the catastrophe that is often synonymous with revelation.

There is a correlation of the intricate and fragile, of honeycomb structures in unconscious phantasy of a potential axial significance that anticipate the development of an ability to transform matière into art, including the gift of language and of speech. The tower is a representation of such a fragile and unconscious structuring as it centres within the mind of the infant as well as of its mother. An inheritance is reflected in a shared gaze. Whatever it is that brings about spiritual growth in the interaction of the nurturing dyad cannot be accessed. The tower exists in each of us – in the nurtured baby as well as in the breast that feeds it. Through a correlation of structures of this kind silence is able to transform matière into art. Within each of us exists from before the beginning, as a precursor to articulation, a delicate and growing structure, a prototype of the tower or the bronze half-sphere. In the shiny bronze surface of the sculpture I see the gaze as a means of communication. But disintegration can happen, and the artist may be faced by incoherence. Silence begins to assert itself as "a live and immediate revelation of the unfathomable", which is how Goethe thought of the symbol (Maxim 314, in Stopp & Hutchinson, 1998: 37). Silence is the one language out of which manifold tongues take on being. It is without place; it is everywhere and nowhere. Concepts of inward and outward, or near and far, have no bearing on it. I may contemplate it by turning to a mantra or a mandala as a means of focus, but without it these means are void of value. Silence is not an absence of hearing. It is auditory perception of a certain kind.[3]

When I think of the stillness of great painting, and of the silence in this stillness, I am aware of a contradiction: that I am responding to the visual as though it were sound. In great art the silence of the visual is more than an absence of noise or sound. The contemplation of the artist in an act of making translates into a depth in silence that may possess the spectator. A meditative power exists in the painting. There is a palpable communication of reminiscence, which is the

---

[3] One of the Brahmin priests in certain Vedic rituals is identified with silence. He speaks only to correct errors in the recitation of other priests. The effect of his silence is to draw attention to the fact that silence charges the meaning of words. It imbues the spoken word with the numinous. It indicates that the relation of a rite of this kind to the cosmos, although real, in its perplexity is no different from the exchange of riddles in certain jousts practised by the priests (Renou & Silburn, 1949).

history of a process of making that has survived without the aid of time or space. Something is set apart that is unrelated to the actual. I think of the paintings in the National Gallery in London: I could equally well think of any other great collection. The paintings cast a light on the phantasms of those who flit by beneath them; they enhance dimensionality and endow bodies and faces with an unaccustomed beauty. Should I think of this light as a way in which the imaginary transforms experience? I think of radiance as an aspect of the silence that is present when I look at the paintings. The radiance is gentle. The silence cannot be denied.

The sacrality of art – that is, the presence of the act of sacrifice in art – is daunting. Fatigue and a desire to retreat from the experience can assail anyone on approach to the gallery entrance. Something is about to happen that the conscious mind cannot register. The space of the streets and buildings outside the gallery fades away as a mysterious and momentous space opens up within. There is a sense of the vast. Why should paintings be able to transform the space about them? A space is a shrine to silence, in spite of the many who throng about within it.

In aesthetics a depth in silence is a ground to the intolerable, as well as to greatness. Think of the speed with which an audience finds relief from the silence at a performance's end by its thundering applause. A silence can be overwhelming and even unbearable when there is a ban on applause at the end of sacred performance. The archaic and the superstitious are unconcealed. I wonder what it would be like to spend a night alone in the company of these paintings. Does silence in darkness withdraw into the paintings? Does the meaning of the sacrifice become apparent? "Alone . . . he approached the very darkness itself. . . . He was in the company of the Invisible" (Gregory of Nyssa, writing about Moses, in Malherbe & Ferguson, 1978: 43).

Some time after my visit to Rotterdam, I had the opportunity to look at Bruegel's earlier treatment of the tower theme in the Vienna Kunsthistorisches Museum. With Genesis, and even more firmly with later commentators like Josephus, the building of the tower is a subject for disapproval. But Bruegel is a non-judgmental painter. His approach to the tower is without condemnation. It just is, and in its materiality it is a symbol for nothing other than itself. It is no different, in its incompleteness or state of damage, from a human body that has passed its prime. In the Vienna tower, it would seem that the builders can scarcely keep up in their work with an increasing state of deterioration. In this painting human artefacts grow out of nature and never quite leave its confines and so, like objects in nature, are disposed to physical transience. While the Rotterdam tower is gaunt, even ecclesiastical in impression – it communicates the awesome silence of a cathedral interior by moonlight – the Vienna tower brings to mind Kafka's droll perception of inertia as a general human principle.

> It was the general opinion at the time that one could not build too slowly; this opinion needed to be over-emphasised a little and people would have shrunk from laying the foundations at all. . . . By the time of the second or third generation the senselessness of building a tower up to the heaven was already recognised, but by that time everybody was far too closely bound up with one another to leave the city. . . . All the legends and songs that have originated in this city are filled with longing for a prophesied day, on which the city will be smashed to pieces by five blows in rapid succession from a gigantic fist. That is why the city has a fist on its coat of arms.
>
> [KAFKA, *THE CITY COAT OF ARMS*, IN PASLEY, 1973: 120–121]

A massive presence looms up too closely to the picture surface and yet without overwhelming a never-ending greenish plain that is more typical of Flanders than of the valley of Shinar. The great city of Babel behind the tower appears to be half-asleep, while the boats that lie at anchor are without a sense of Renaissance verve. The tower reveals evidence in its deterioration that it might have been carved out of a mountain. Rocks show through in two places. The incomplete higher levels (or perhaps the higher levels are more collapsed than incomplete) expose a precisely constructed series of shapes, whose reddish hue resembles the exposing of entrails in one of Rembrandt's anatomy-class paintings. The tower lists to one side. In an intimation of disaster, a small house next to it is half-immersed in what appears to be the waters of a flood. Natural process makes more sense of this deterioration than any idea of divine condemnation. Bruegel's impassivity is of a piece with his sense of irony. I do not believe that the figure in the foreground, who may be Nimrod as the patron of the tower (but who can be sure?), is held up to ridicule.

Implicit in the fascination of Bruegel's two depictions of the tower is the covert power of a geometry that is spiritual rather than secular, and that draws the mind into its depths. A similar effect is to be found in the Buddhist mandala or the Hindu yantra and in images of the labyrinth. The tower is similar to the "ladder" of Jacob's dream on which angels move up and down. The angels could freely ascend as well as descend if the ladder, like the tower, had ramps rather than rungs. William Blake, in one of his pictures, has a similar perception of Jacob's ladder as a wide staircase.

Genesis draws an etymological parallel between the naming of the tower and of Babylon itself and the babble and confusion of tongues. But Joseph Blenkinsopp (2011: 167) has questioned this etymology. In Akkadian, *bab ili* signifies the gate of heaven or the gate of the gods. Jacob, in waking from his dream, observes: "How dreadful is this place. This is none other than the house of God and this is the gate of heaven." The significance of the theophany is different in either case. The building of the tower involves effort, like the building of the fire altar, and Harland (1998) may be right in thinking that the deity wished to release his people from the enclosure of an ivory tower by the scattering of tongues. But the silent imagery of Jacob's dream is a spiritual endowment. In the generosity of its giving it involves no effort on the part of the recipient. As in dreams, so it is in a silence that evades its role as the silence of the sacrifice and creates for itself a different symbol.

It must be immense, this silence, in which sounds and
movements have room, and if one thinks that along with all
this the presence of the distant sea also resounds, perhaps
as the innermost note in this prehistoric harmony, then one
can only wish that you are trustingly and patiently letting
the magnificent solitude work upon you, this solitude which
can no longer be erased from your life; which, in everything
that is in store for you to experience and to do, will act as
an anonymous influence, continuously and gently decisive,
rather as the blood of our ancestors incessantly moves in us
and combines with our own to form the unique, unrepeatable
being that we are at every turning of our life.
[RAINER MARIA RILKE, IN MITCHELL, 1984: 106–107]

I have before me the reproduction of the "Annunciation" by
Fra Filippo Lippi; the painting is in London, in the National
Gallery. Allegedly at one time the painting was situated in a
lunette above a doorway: but architectural expedience apart,
the gently curving arch to the top of the painting provides a
sense of shelter to the two figures in the portico beneath it. On
the right of the painting kneels a young man, and before him,
on the other side of the painting, is seated a young woman.
Between them and above them a hand stretches down
from beyond the edge of the painting and releases a faintly
visible dove.

In Luke 1: 26–28, the young man, who is the angel
Gabriel, speaks to the young woman. He is the messenger.

Here he is something more. The silence between the couple signals the deepest intimacy. This is a representation of love at first sight.[1] Neither figure looks at the other. Eyes and heads are lowered. The couple have scarcely left the state of puberty, and their beauty and grace is feminine. The painter, in making them each for the other, has given them identical haloes of a faded golden hue that in shape reflects the arching top to the painting. Their ample cloaks fold into many creases as they touch the surface of the ground. The pattern of the folds of one cloak sets up a pattern in harmony with the folds of the other. The colour of his pale red cloak is identical to the pale red colour of her dress, but the blue of her cloak is noticeably different from the grey of his vestments. The curve of his feathered wings is like the arch of the picture edge above them. He is the archangel Gabriel, who brings life to Mary, who in turn receives the Son of God in her womb through the silence of the angel. She, Mary, "is the silence that incarnates" (Lossky, 1978: 90). Mary personifies the ability of the contemplative mind to introject. In paintings, she is often seen to be reading a book.

> If anyone were to ask nature why it makes, it might answer: You ought not to ask but to understand in silence, just as I am silent. What comes into being is what I see in my silence, an object of contemplation that comes to be naturally and that I, originating from this sort of contemplation have a contemplative nature. And my act of contemplation makes what it

[1] Silence is the link in love at first sight. In psychoanalytic terms, it is all that I can know of that which combines the combined object as the source of sanity.

contemplates, as the geometers draw their figures while they contemplate. But I do not draw, but as I contemplate, the lines that bound bodies come to be as if they fell from my contemplation.

[PLOTINUS, *ENNEAD III* 8.4, IN ARMSTRONG, 1967]

The silence of Gabriel is the silence of the Holy Spirit that releases the Word within the womb: this is what it means to say that the mind has opened itself to silence without any desire for gain. The silence of the painting forms the vibrant space that holds the couple together.

> [The] pregnant space is not new to painting. One need only think of Simone Martini's incredibly beautiful painting from 1333 of the Annunciation in the Uffizi in Florence. Flanked on the left side by the Archangel Gabriel and on the right by the unsuspecting Virgin, the empty central area of the painting is, literally, pregnant with expectation. Perhaps related to this is a sense of time. For paintings are as much about holding time, their own time, as they are about form and space. The time it takes for apparently empty, abstract space to begin to hold potential meaning or the waiting for meaning to configure itself. Of course, wedded to this is also a sense of stillness, a slowing down. Have you noticed how fast-painted pictures are seldom quiet, rarely hold still? Adrian Stokes once wrote, "The great work of art is surrounded by silence.
>
> [MCKEEVER, 2015: 54–55]

The space between the couple is the factor that is in-between, which Aristotle excludes in his celebrated law of the excluded middle. To deny Aristotle his law is to exclude the values of negation. The imagination originates in the absence of the excluded middle as it gives form to the symbol. The angel's gift carries with it the meaning of the act of sacrifice that the Word represents. Every receptive mind is open to the grief of this mother. She is *theotokos*, the bearer of the divine presence.[2]

[2] "She who by the power of the Holy Spirit received the divine person of the Son of God into her womb, [on the day of the Pentecost] receives the Holy Spirit sent by her Son" (Lossky, 1949: 206).

In her diaries, Simone Weil refers three times to silence: "*Le Verbe est le silence de Dieu*" (Diary 1941–1942, in Devaux & de Lussy, 1997: 373). "*Le Verbe, silence de Dieu, parole dans la creation*" (ibid.: 374). "*Le silence de Dieu nous contraint au silence intérieur*" (ibid.: 392). The Word is the silence of God. It is the occurrence of speech in the created world. It draws the mind towards a silence that is inward. The Holy Spirit as silence and the Word as the manifestation of form in the world derive in different ways from the unknowable. In the mystical theology of the Eastern Church, the Father begets the Word as his Son and, separately from this act of engenderment, enables the Holy Spirit to proceed from Him. A theology of this kind celebrates the act by which form is embodied. It differs from the understanding of Plato and his followers, who feel disquiet at the world of matter and seek to deny it any merit. The act of embodiment in this theology is luminous with the presence of the Holy Spirit.

> Our analysis leads us finally towards the Truth and the Spirit, the Word and the Holy Spirit, two persons distinct but indissolubly united, whose twofold economy, while founding the Church, conditions at the same time the indissoluble and distinct character of Scripture and Tradition.
>
> [LOSSKY, 1959: 152–153]

> In its pure notion there is nothing formal [to Tradition]. It does not impose on human consciousness formal guarantees of the truths of faith, but it gives access to the discovery of their inner evidence. It is not the content of Revelation, but the light that reveals it; it is not the Word but the living breath which makes the words heard at the same time as the silence from which it came; it is not the Truth, but a communication of the Spirit of Truth, outside which the Truth cannot be received. . . . The pure notion of Tradition can be defined by saying that it is the life of the Holy Spirit in the Church, communicating to each member of the Body of Christ the faculty of hearing, of receiving, of knowing the Truth in the light which belongs to it, and not according to the natural light of human reason.
>
> [IBID.: 151–152]

Tradition represents the critical spirit of the Church. But contrary to the critical spirit of human science, the critical judgment of the Church is made acute by the Holy Spirit.

[IBID.: 156]

Tradition tells us not only what we must hear but, still more importantly, how we keep what we hear. In this general sense, Tradition implies an incessant outpouring of the Holy Spirit, who could have his full outpouring and bear his fruits only in the Church, after the Day of Pentecost.

[LOSSKY, 1949: 198]

The theologian Olivier Clément kept notes while attending lectures that Lossky gave in Paris in 1957.

Lossky liked to point out the difference between the presence of the Word and the presence of the Spirit. The Word is Logos; it determines and gives structure; it measures out. It provides order and stability. At the beginning it is reason, causality, the norm, the objective, while the Holy Spirit is life, participation, becoming, the subjective. The Holy Spirit is Pneuma or breath; it restores to life. It enables plenitude to exist and it informs achievement: it is force, momentum and dynamism. The Word is the divine energy of Creation while the Spirit is the same energy as a luminous penetration. . . . The Word "locates" the creative impulse. The Spirit is the force, the light and the glory that accompanies the beauty of ideas.

[CLÉMENT, 1985: 62-63]

Human understanding is unable to trace directly the relation between inspiration and the coming into being of form. An unknowable of inconceivable magnitude gives rise to each of them in separate ways. Only by an intuition of that which cannot be known can the contemplator sense a correlation between inspiration and form. The symbol is inaccessible if measure is the one perspective. It is accessible as a mandala or a templum if the perspective is the immeasurable. The silence of an angel engenders the child in this womb.

Darkness upon darkness/gateway to the subtle.
[TAO TE CHING, CH. 1]

Plato's demiurge extracts time and space out of eternity
in a process of transformation in which there is neither a
secure definition of time and space nor a secure definition
of eternity. Concepts like negation or beginning or ending
are unsecured. Measure is unstable and unpredictable. A
psychologist might see here an interim stage in the formation
of psychic life; a theologian might see here a realm of angels; a
performer of ritual might see here a place where the sacrifice
is most meaningful; and a Romantic poet might see this place
as relevant to the forming of the symbol. This is where the
symbol forms as it enters time and space. It has no beginning
and no end and no source and no destination. In radiance it
hovers. Acts of making in the narratives of creation are not

evidential acts of making as they might be in the active life. They are not founded in an empiricism that is inseparable from the coinage of evidence. All of them aspire to be the symbol.

Silence is a prototype for the gift of any thought that is not base or discouraging. Thoughts are in no way objects made as they manifest themselves. They are always gifts. If I think of eternity as the unfathomable depths of mind, and the act of forming time and space as an interaction between a foetal and nurturing identity, then the notion of a gift (in which the identity of the giver and the identity of the receiver is veiled) replaces the notion of an act of making. The vagueness of the concept of "beginning", as in the narrative of creation, is one that must trouble anyone who attempts to interpret the meaning of the symbol. Silence informs the acts of creation as the Holy Spirit in the womb of the mother. It informs the narratives of creation as the immeasurable in the womb of the father. In the womb of the mother there is a sense of expectation, like a room filling with sunlight. In the womb of the father there is darkness and little more than traces of light. The darkness that Russell's balloon moves through does not supply the traveller with a sense of orientation. As in the creation narrative of Plato's *Timaeus*, it exists between the eternal and the formation of time and space. This is the time and place of sacrifice. Any evidence of measure is insubstantial and unpredictable. The traveller requires a thinker of Einstein's calibre to decipher anything. In the narrative of creation, the womb of the father can communicate the beauty, as well as the dread, of a darkness that cannot be explained.

In the beginning, according to the *Rig Veda*,

Non-Being did not exist nor Being.
The space known as air did not exist nor the heavens
beyond.
What was it that moved so powerfully?
And from where?
And under whose guidance?
Was there water unfathomable, profound?

[RIG VEDA, 129: 10]

What was it that moved so powerfully in the dark and
formless infinite of the father's womb? A similar question
appears in the creation narrative of Laozi's *Tao Te Ching*.
Laozi's scepticism concerning the values of human communication reflects the metaphysical darkness of the generative
space within the father that is his womb, even though Laozi
discovers the metaphysical source to life within the microcosm of a mother's womb.

[An] aura of depth and urgency pervades the
pronouncements of the *Tao Te Ching*. Devoid of
context, with all superfluous syntax and connec-
tives lopped away, they stand like so many stone
inscriptions, peering out at us from a mysterious and
shadowy place. . . . It is this numinous and evasive
quality in the text that accounts for its perennial appeal. The words do not readily yield up their
message but seem to recede further into obscurity the
more assiduously one struggles with them.

[WATSON, 1993: XXIX]

The way that can be spoken of
Is not the constant way:
The name that can be named
Is not the constant name.
The nameless was the beginning of the heaven and earth;
The name was the mother of myriad creatures.

[*TAO TE CHING*, IN LAU, 1963: 57]

Language in relation to the *Tao* must crumble and in time disappear and take with it every understanding. If I were to modify the ferocious interpretation of Genesis 11, I might say that the *Tao* holds the Tower of Babel in its embrace, as eternity and time and space communicate with each other.

Truth in the father's womb can be scarcely recognised. Something is missing. The opening pages of the book no longer exist. Questions raised by the damaged text cannot be answered. There is darkness. In birth each life uniquely, and once and once only, wavers between life and death. In the early stages, any differentiation of subject and object is unsure, and any idea of place is a promise rather than a fulfilment. Everything glimmers in so far as it is anything: incipient thoughts are realised or disappear. The contours of later experience reflect this state of apprehension. In fable a woman who felt rejected by the magician Merlin confined him in a cube-shaped room whose walls were made of air: the contours of experience are similar. As the years pass, there may be intimations of earlier narratives. A visionary dimension that pre-exists the forming of worlds may present itself as "a perpetual possibility in a world of speculation. . . .

Footfalls echo in the memory / Down the passage we did not take / Towards the door we never opened" (Eliot, 1936: 7).

The foetus, bathed in the radiance of silence, finds itself born into an Aristotelian world that observes the law of the excluded middle. "Nothing" rather than "something" lies between "is" and "is not". There is a stage in the forming of space and time out of eternity, in which there is no stable means of measure. What Plato describes in macrocosmic terms through his personification of intelligence as a demiurge applies equally to the microcosm of the individual mind. Out of unfathomable depths eternity informs space and time. The darkness that Russell's balloon passes through signifies a processual idea of negation in which measure is unstable. The concept of beginning follows a similar semantic path as it marks the origination of active life. In the contemplative life there is no beginning and end. A mind in contemplation discovers that silence has always been there. It is as it were before any beginning and after any end. The concept of selfhood like the concept of beginning is essential in helping us to pass through life. It is, however, misleading in relation to silence. It is on this point that revelation and the imagination move towards a definition. And yet the two are very different.

Outside of revelation nothing is known of the difference
between the increate and the created.

[LOSSKY, 1944: 32]

Vladimir Lossky thinks of revelation as a means of communication between the increate and the created. Samuel Taylor
Coleridge has a similar idea about the imagination. The
essential difference is that Lossky believes that Revelation
is synonymous with the meaning of the Incarnation as the
Word made Flesh. Coleridge signally excludes any mention
of the Incarnation in his definition of the imagination in the
Biographia Literaria. He looks, rather, to the Genesis creation
narrative and correlates its effect with the visionary moment
in which Moses looks into the flames of the burning bush.
The influence of the Milton of *Paradise Lost* weighs heavily. It
is never fully absorbed.

The correlation of the Genesis creation narrative with

the burning bush incident occurs within the primary imagi-nation, which is "the living power and prime agent of all human perception . . . a representation in the finite mind of the eternal act of creation in the infinite I AM" (Coleridge, 1817b: 167). Re-defining the enigmatic meaning of the voice in the bush (I AM that I AM) as the infinite I AM enables Coleridge to lift the Genesis creation narrative into a Platonic state of timelessness. The secondary imagination is a deriva-tive of the primary imagination, but quite how is not clear. It "dissolves, diffuses, dissipates, in order to re-create; or where this process is rendered impossible, yet still, in all events, it struggles to idealize and to unify. It is essentially vital, even as all objects (as objects) are essentially fixed and dead" (ibid.). Opening mind to the increate differs greatly from the cerebral type of connection-making that Coleridge derogates as "fancy". The secondary imagination is bound to the primary imagina-tion and would not survive without it. It sees the imagination is an endowment and not a mental faculty; and according to the Holy Spirit it appears and disappears.

A quotation from Milton's *Paradise Lost* (5.469–488) provides the chapter on imagination with one of its epigraphs. The archangel Raphael defines reason to Adam as a commu-nication between the increate and the created world that endows with spiritual life the objects in the created world. The spiritual nurtures the bright flower, as much as do the nutrients of soil, warmth and air. In a similar way, it nurtures human interaction. To considerable effect, Coleridge quotes from – or, rather, misquotes – Synesius, a fourth-century bishop of Cyrenaica. "Music of the mind, (*Synesius wrote of mysteries rather than of music) /* speak of this thing and that, / your inexpressible depths / are what we dance around" (Coleridge, 1817b: 162n). Synesius wrote: "I venerate the hidden order of things." The conception of reason in this case is one to be associated with the name of Plato and his followers and not with the names of Bacon and Descartes. Fundamental to the distinction is an age-old problem that applies as much to the creative process as it does to religion: that the resources that enable the self to acquire knowledge are unable to communicate the hidden order of things that Synesius venerates.

The paradigm of the creationist narrative is the loom on which the poet is witness to the weaving of the symbol. The ways of the symbol are as incomprehensible as are the ways in which the creationist narrative unfolds. The symbol is like a dream image in its emanation. It forms as its own evidence in spite of any darkness. Like the creationist narrative, it calls on an act of faith. Any attempt to engage with it must be troubled by doubt. A certain depth and resonance is known by means of silence alone.

> The symbol is not an artificially constructed sign. It flowers in the soul spontaneously to announce something that cannot be expressed otherwise; it is the unique expression of the thing symbolised as of a reality that thus becomes transparent to the soul but which in itself transcends all expression. . . . To penetrate to the meaning of the symbol is in no sense to make it superfluous or to abolish it, for it always remains the sole expression of the signified thing that it

> symbolises. One can never claim to have gone beyond
> it once and for all, save at the cost of degrading it into
> an allegory, of putting rational, general and abstract
> equivalences in its place.
>
> [CORBIN, 1954: 30][1]

The effect of bringing the angelic form inside the flame and the voice within the glowing branches into the Genesis creation narrative is numinous. Coleridge gives the enigmatic voice a Platonic touch by naming it the "infinite I AM". Within the father's womb, as in this case, the tone of the prophet is uncertain. "Entering into a pure loss of self, the soul finds God in Nothingness. A man had a waking dream, that he was great with Nothingness as a woman is with child. In this Nothingness God was born. He was the fruit of Nothingness. God was born in Nothingness" (Meister Eckhart, in McGinn, 1981: 10). "The image is an emanation from the depths of a silence that excludes everything that comes from without" (Meister Eckhart, in McGinn, 2001: 72). Revelation breaks into the created world by a specific act of sacrificing the self.

Coleridge presumes that conscious realisation, if it is to have depth, is inseparable from an otherwise inaccessible source. I may be unable to dream about the angelic ladder that Jacob perceived, but I may turn to Jacob's dream to discover an unworldly element that lies in every poetic. "All truth is a

---

[1] There is the life that I live and a life that lives me out. The life that I live presents itself as the series of variations whose relation to each other I cannot elucidate. The life that lives me out is the symbol I cannot control or explain. I may imagine the life that I live as unending, as though time had made for me an exception to the rule of oblivion. The dictation of the symbol is other. The life that lives me out may cease like the click of a spool that has unwound. The symbol is daunting and desired, and it can be opaque or lucid. It rises as the lotus out of darkened waters.

species of revelation", wrote Coleridge in a letter to Thomas Poole (27 March, 1801). The telescope that looks outwards is the telescope that looks inwards. In an age more self-consciously psychological than the age of the prophets, Coleridge looks to nature to confirm a truth that is self-reflective.

> Saturday Night April 14, 1805 – In looking at the objects of nature, while I am thinking, as at yonder moon dim-glimmering thro' the dewy window-pane, I seem rather to be seeking, as it were asking, a symbolic language for something within me that already and forever exists, than observing any thing new. Even when that latter is the case, yet still I have always an obscure feeling as if that new phaenomenon were the dim Awaking of a forgotten or hidden Truth of my inner Nature / It is still interesting as a Word, a Symbol! It is the Logos (*in Greek*), the Creator.
>
> [COLERIDGE, IN COBURN, 1961, ENTRY 2546]

Coleridge compares the "self-intuition" of the primary imagination – in other words, the moment before the burning bush – to those

> who within themselves can interpret and understand the symbol, that the wings of the air-sylph are forming within the skin of the caterpillar; those only who feel in their own spirits the same instinct, which impels the chrysalis of the horned fly to leave room in its involucrum for antennae yet to come. They know and feel that the potential works in them, even as the actual works on them!
>
> [COLERIDGE, 1817A: 241–242]

Creationist narratives belong to the same order of being as the symbol. Their claim to be historical events is as unworldly as is the claim that the time that Plato's demiurge extracts from eternity might be other than angelic. The pulse that arises out of the increate is luminous and unspecific. The parts of measure extracted from it are in a more primitive form the parts of a body in sacrifice.

> In the beginning God created the heaven and the earth. And the earth was without form, and void; and darkness was upon the face of the deep. And the Spirit of God moved upon the face of the waters. And God said, Let there be light: and there was light. And God saw the light, that it was good: and God divided the light from the darkness.
>
> [GENESIS 1: 2–3]

The light that the divine presence summons up in the Genesis creation narrative does not initiate sunrise. It does not exist in nature. It is as inconceivable as the light greater than a thousand suns of the *Bhagavad Gita*. The series of creative acts in in the Genesis narrative is unlike any human act of creation. It is a-temporal while marking itself out in time. To follow Coleridge, it is an enunciation of "I AM that I AM". The light and the void are bound together in the heart of the founding principle. The narrative says nothing about the Word. Or, rather, the Word is everywhere, if not seen, within the silence that conjoins the light and the void.

"The earth was without form and void, and darkness was upon the face of the deep."

Tōhu bōhu or *Tōhu vavōhu* is the void in Hebrew. *Tōhu* signifies nothingness as well as the void, while *Bōhu* signifies emptiness as well as desolation. The light of a theophany in the desert is also the void. The alien enters the familiar. Time and space, dispossessed, are at a loss concerning the original vision. There is catastrophe in the interaction between the increate and the created: this is revelation. There is reconciliation as the divine presence looks on the face of the waters: otherwise the intensity of the light that is the void passes understanding. The powers that disintegrate as they integrate and integrate as they disintegrate are a factor in the origination of the creative act. Nature at its most awesome does no more than marginally reflect the generative powers of the increate. "To perish in the howling infinite", thought Herman Melville (1851: 103). It is like a painting by J.M.W. Turner. A subterranean sea, whose size and depth is incalculable, forms out of the conjoining of the light and the void. It disables experience. "The rising world of waters dark and deep" that John Milton thinks of as "won from the void and formless infinite" (*Paradise Lost* 3. 11–12) resists any return to its source. The created can only signal meanings in terms of the increate. It cannot rediscover its beginnings. Means of communication disappear in any movement towards the conjoining of the light and the void; language buckles, and the enchantment of music recedes.

The primary imagination as an idea stirs restlessness in

the created world. The prophet turns from the richness of the world and expects to find traces of otherness in the wilderness. Anchorites look to desert wastes for a yearned-for absence. Nomads are attracted to the solitude of the immeasurable; they rest within the silence that existed before the first dawn. The desert is where the prophet Isaiah (13: 21) thought that ostriches dwelt and satyrs danced.

> Darkness was common to the three interrelated realms of the ocean, the desert and death. One day God would prevail over them. . . . The ocean was an awesome reminder of the primordial chaos that lies lurking under the world of man and that like the desert is the haunt of serpents and dragons.
>
> [WILLIAMS, 1962: 14]

The floor of the sea lightly covers the abyss. The ninth-century theologian John Scotus Eriugena identified the desert or ocean with the unfathomable nature of the divine presence (McGinn, 1994: 163). Baitan, who was a friend of St Columba, attempted "to seek a desert in the ocean" (*Adomnan's Life of St Columba*, in McGinn, 1994: 163). Dionysius, in the *Celestial Hierarchy* 9.3, refers to "the limitless and bounteous ocean of the divine light" (in Luibheid, 1987: 171–172). In a disquieting vision "We wonder at the open sea and its limitless depth; but we wonder fearfully when we stoop down and see how deep it is. It was in this way that the Psalmist stooped down [referring to Ps. 138: 6 and 141] and looked at the limitless yawning sea of God's wisdom [*to apeiron . . . pelagos tēs tou theou sophias*]. He was struck with shuddering." (St John

Chrysostom, in McGinn, 1994: 159).

A stranger on returning home may fail to be recognised. Or the stranger may have difficulty in seeing that the place arrived at is home. In relation to the increate, the concept of location falls apart as it is about to form. Within the womb of the Father, the void and the light, as brides of the divine presence, form into the embodied. Means of communication fragment and disappear as a return to the increate takes place. Intimacy in relation to the Word is inseparable from the vast.

The assumption that the symbol appears without explanation, out of an unknown pulse, conflicts with the need to justify the existence of the symbol by turning to an ancestral text. The unfathomable presents itself to the mind of the poet, or to the forming of foetal consciousness, in ways that the understanding is unable to register. But the increate can and does enter the created world. In its loneliness, the voice within the burning bush requires someone to speak to. Only a certain kind of listener has the aptitude to hear it: the stranger, the one who is unrecognised, Moses. The light and the void conjoin within the glowing embers of the fire of inspiration. In the womb of the mother, a vision of this kind is related to the grace of silence – in the womb of the father, to a darkness that disorientates. Moses must recognise, in part only and in anguish, a truth that is comparable to the traces of light seen from Russell's balloon. Here there can be no knowledge. The grid of time and space is yet to assert itself. The fire within the bush neither devours the twigs, nor do the twigs devour the fire. The burning, which is indefinite, is like the circularity in self-definition of the voice that speaks from within it. Orders of succession are obscured.

The awe of Moses is unlike the Platonic sense of wonder, which co-exists with a sense of otherness. It is immediate in its sense of the here and now. There is no escape into past or future. There is only an eternal presence that cannot be entered. The omniscience that characterises the creation narratives of Genesis or of the *Timaeus* leave it untouched. Moses is an isolated and by nature timid figure. "Moses was very meek, above all men which were upon the face of the earth" (Numbers 12: 3). He is one who "trembles with fear where no fear is" (Psalm 13). He is well ordered for the visionary life. Withdrawn, dispossessed, denied a sense of fulfilment or of identity, he must be born in obscurity and be buried in an unknown grave. In the not knowing of where he comes from and where he is to go to, he reflects the logic by which the symbol forms. His virtue lies in a nomadic yearning.[2] He names his son Gershom because he, the father, was a stranger in a strange land (Exodus 2: 22). He lives in doubt. He comes from afar. He would, if he could, retire into nowhere as nobody, if the inscrutable voice did not summon him.

The symbol in its emergence can be tantalisingly opaque. It can be destructive. It can cause stillness to fall on the hand of the potter. It can leave the poet bereft of words. The disorder of tongues is not a punishment, as the architect of the Tower

---

[2] Marcel Mauss described the life of the nomad as "an act of faith" (Mauss, 1926, : 531). Recent scholarship has called into doubt the attractive assumption that the early Israelites were nomads who turned away from local nature cults and in the emptiness of the desert found the God of history (see Hiebert, 1996).

of Babel must have realised. It is a response to a certain type of privileged reality. The fire of the burning bush intimates the existence of a conjoined void and light that in destroying everything can bring into existence a created world of many tongues. I may learn to speak a thousand languages, and yet there are always more. And there are languages beyond speech, like the babble or cry or the utterances of silence. In Donald Meltzer's view (personal communication), a patient in psychoanalysis may be at a loss for words or stumble in speech or stutter because of some proximity to the otherwise unknowable presence of the unconscious combined object. Language in this circumstance presents itself as a way of linking the two parts of the combined object as a metaphor that would as a symbolic force exclude the isolated individual. The intensity of thinking without a thought, which is one definition of contemplative silence, is inseparable from a type of creative incoherence. Consider the following thoughts:

> A poet, essayist or philosopher may be trying hard to find the word, phrase or argument that he needs, but the time when he is thinking what to say is the time when he still has nothing to say. In some thinking, the soul is only stammering to itself.
>
> [RYLE, 1951: 69]

> Looking intently is difficult. It's possible to look intently without seeing anything, or to keep thinking you see something without being able to see clearly. Looking can tire you even when you don't see anything.
>
> [LUDWIG WITTGENSTEIN, IN MONK, 1990: 537]

We may say that it has to do with a state of mind in which insight may come rather than with the content of insight.

[DOROTHY EMMET, 1966: 52]

... many individuals think they are not praying when, indeed, their prayer is deep.

[ST JOHN OF THE CROSS, IN KAVANAUGH & RODRIGUES, 1966: 117]

The field that the pilgrim enters may present itself as similar to the darkness that Russell's balloon travels through. A breakdown in the concept of place may intimate an apophatic presence. An experience that no one registers can be an experience nonetheless, as in the case of revelation. I may experience silence as a benevolent endowment that co-exists with the pulse of breathing. Again vaguely, unsurely, and yet with a sense of portent, I may find that I associate this presence to a certain catastrophe that cannot be located in event or measure. Intuitions of this kind may be identified with a twin, possibly imaginary, that dies at birth. Within silence a theophany can emerge that hopefully the one who dies in stillbirth may know. The Egyptian god Osiris was known as the Lord of silence. His wife–sister Isis sought everywhere for his bodily parts after his dismemberment in an act of sacrifice. In some legends she never found his penis; in other legends, and in a variant on the idea of the Annunciation, she found the penis and was able to practise an act of self-insemination on herself. In time she gave birth to Horus as the first king of Egypt. Out of darkness, emerged the first king.

The source of inspiration within the poet cannot be communicated: the Genesis creation narrative – indeed, every creation narrative – is little more than an approximation for this source. Primary imagination impels into action the secondary imagination, and the symbol comes into being. The unimaginable energy of the void/light of the increate bring into existence the created. Within the glowing embers, a voice offers itself up as the infinite I AM. A symbol begins to emerge. In the age of reason philosophers will turn to the theory of the sublime as an admission that the understanding must fail in circumstances of this kind. The sublime is a presentiment of the Romantic symbol. It is a type of dis-articulation. For the man of reason, it is like being choked at birth.

[Moses] breaks free from [the holy places], away from what sees and is seen, and plunges into the truly mysterious darkness of unknowing. . . . Here, being neither himself nor someone else, he is supremely united by a completely unknowing inactivity of all knowledge, and knows beyond the mind by knowing nothing.

[PSEUDO-DIONYSUS, IN LUIBHEID, 1987: 137]

What does it mean to say that Moses entered the darkness?

[GREGORY OF NYSSA, IN MALHERBE & FERGUSON, 1978: 94]

The Mystical Theology of Dionysius (in Luibheid, 1987: 131–141) consists of seven pages of text and a page of two letters relevant to its theme.[1] The text and the two letters have had a transformatory influence over St Thomas Aquinas and Meister Eckhart, among many others. On the threshold between the increate and the created, communication is synonymous with the logic of contradiction.[2] In terms of

[1] There is no certain evidence for the claim that Dionysius was a fifth-century Syrian monk.

[2] The oxymoron itself is oxymoronic in its etymology. "Oxy" in medical usage among the ancient Greeks signifies excessively acute or sensitive, and "moron" signifies dull, foolish or stupid. Examples of the oxymoron: A single sesame seed (among the Sufis) generates innumerable worlds. A mother looks into a young child's mouth and discovers there the constellations of infinite worlds. (This is the mother of the god Krishna.)

figures of speech, the oxymoron replaces the metaphor. The oxymoron yokes together meanings by way of a contradiction. Dionysius uses it as a figure of speech to describe the apophatic ascent. "My argument now rises from what is below up to the transcendent, and the more it climbs, the more language falters, and when it has passed up and beyond the ascent, it will turn silent completely, since it will finally be at one with Him who is indescribable" (Dionysius, in Luibheid, 1987: 139). The brilliant darkness (an oxymoron) is of a hidden silence (another oxymoron). Dionysius advises a fellow monk, Timothy, to give up "everything perceived and understood . . . and by an undivided and absolute abandonment of yourself and everything . . . you will be uplifted to the ray of divine shadow" (in Luibheid, 1987: 135). I find this insight as far beyond my understanding as I do Wilfred Bion's use of a beam of darkness (also an oxymoron) to sound the depths of transference. And yet this way of thinking impresses me as meaningful.[3]

"Plunge", the verb that Colm Luibheid uses in his translation of Dionysius, describes an entry into what appears to be Milton's "rising world of waters dark and deep won from the void and formless infinite". The primary imagination when isolated from the created world is able to contract any

---

[3] On an incompatibility between insight and intellect see St John of the Cross. "When the divine light of contemplation strikes a soul not yet entirely illumined, it causes spiritual darkness, for it not only surpasses the act of natural understanding but it also deprives the soul of this act and darkens it. This is why Dionysius and other mystical theologians call this infused contemplation a 'ray of darkness' – that is, for the soul not yet illumined and purged. For this great supernatural light overwhelms the intellect and deprives it of its natural vigour" (St John of the Cross, in Kavanaugh & Rodriguez, 1966: 402).

evidence of the secondary imagination into itself. It replaces reassurance with an analogue for the howling infinite of Herman Melville. Mind in the contemplative life operates by way of description. It distrusts any attempt at explanation. In the contemplative life Russell's description of the traveller in the balloon as seeing traces of light is valid, while the attempt at explanation is invalid. The darkness gives no inclination to explain itself.

Moses' ascent of the mountain (it is uncertain whether it is Mount Sinai or Mount Horeb) and his plunge into the "truly mysterious darkness of unknowing" marks a step-by-step denial of the values of the created world. "Here, being neither himself nor someone else, he is supremely united to the completely unknown by a ceasing of all knowledge. He knows beyond the mind by knowing nothing" (Dionysius, in Luibheid, 1987: 137). This eloquent definition of a mystical union anticipates the *ignorantia docta* of St Bonaventure and the "learned ignorance" of Nicolas of Cusa, which Nicolas associated to Socrates' remark that all he knew was that he knew nothing. The darkness that surrounds Moses is not the darkness to which St John of the Cross refers, nor is it the darkness that faced the anonymous author of *The Cloud of Unknowing*. It is not an existential darkness, nor an expression of despair; it does not invoke the topography of a pilgrim; and it has no relation to Bunyan's Slough of Despond. It is a summons, rather, to a darkness that is harsher, cruder and more real than any natural darkness. It is perhaps comparable to the metaphysical rather than psychological darkness that the Swazi people turn to during the Incwala ceremony, in which the king must undergo a symbolic death associated with darkness in order to be restored to the fullness of life. Warriors cover his black skin with a black substance. There is blackness upon blackness, by way of a skin that may fuse with or be separated from the dark night about it. The warriors lead the king into the hut of one of his queens. Hour upon hour the king sits naked and immobile on a lion skin, in a darkness that is darker than any night. The darkness is evocative of Meister Eckhart's "silent desert into which distinction never gazed" (Eckhart, in McGinn, 2001: 72). The subjects of the king have lost any individual identity. There is no coming together and no going apart. Ordinary activities are held in check. Sexual activity is banned. No one can sleep late or touch the other or wash or sit on mats or poke into the ground or scratch their hair. "The identification of the people with the king is total. The spies do not say: you are scratching. They say: you are scratching the king" (Kuper, 1947: 219–220). The sun has set. There is no certainty that it will rise again. The king is identified with an inexpressible force that does not belong to the created world. He undergoes a rite of sacrifice.

Many commentators identify the darkness that Moses plunges into with the thick or dark cloud in which the divine presence conceals itself (Exodus 19:9, 19:16, 24:18). Exodus refers to the darkness only once (20:21) and without any mention of a cloud. The cloud is a means of guidance, while the darkness is incomprehensible.

The Lord went before them in a pillar of cloud by day to guide them along the way and in a pillar of fire by night to give them light, that they might travel day and night. The pillar of cloud by day and the pillar of fire did not depart from before the people.

[EXODUS 13:20]

The cloud leads the Israelites through the desert. It points towards the meaning of the darkness.

> It overshadows all appearances and slowly guides and accustoms the soul to look inwards towards what is hidden. It guides the soul through sense phenomena to the world of the invisible.

[GREGORY OF NYSSA, IN DANIÉLOU, 1962: 24]

> It was no ordinary cloud. It was not composed of vapours or exhalations. It was beyond human comprehension. It was amazing. When the rays of the noonday sun shone with great heat, it was a shelter for the people. It moistened them with dew. During the night it became a fire and from sunset to sunrise led the Israelites in a procession. Moses told his people to keep it in sight.

[GREGORY OF NYSSA, IN MALHERBE & FERGUSON, 1978: 38]

Gregory of Nyssa thinks of every soul as mirroring the cloud, like personalities within a myriad personality reflection. The cloud, as a vehicle of the divine spirit, is similar to the *vihana* or animal vehicle of the Hindu gods. It carries the divine presence to the tabernacle.

> The cloudy-fiery pillar that protected Israel and led them through the wilderness, the same refulgence

that was manifest at Sinai, now rests over and within the Tabernacle as a continuing guarantee of guidance and protection. "Thou goest before them by daytime in a pillar of a cloud and in a pillar of fire by night."

[NUMBERS 14: 14]

Exodus finally explains the nature of the cloud-fire pillar. The cloud is YHWH's vehicle, while the fire is his Glory (compare 24: 17, "the appearance of YHWH's Glory was like a consuming fire", Propp, 2006: 674).

> Cloud and light are in a sense opposites, corresponding to the primal antithesis of dark and light (Genesis 1:2–3). Cloud becomes visible by negating the daylight and fire dispels the night. Yet, in another sense, cloud and fire are complementary since the word used for cloud is a word used for smoke (and the Israelites considered lightning as a form of combustion). The pillar simultaneously evokes images quite distinct for us: a storm cloud and a smoking fire. . . . The precise relationship between the Deity and the pillar is not clear. He seems to be within, or a-top, the pillar. Or the pillar is God or his angelic manifestation. . . . In its bellicose aspect, God's fiery cloudy conveyance recalls stereotypic depictions of the Canaanite God as storm-rider.
>
> [PROPP, 1999: 549–550]

The darkness that Moses plunges into is without orientation; and to think of it as spatial or temporal is to miss its meaning. Moses is unable to speak as he approaches it. There is a negation within body, a state of impending oblivion, an ungovernable fear within the body that that body cannot project out of itself. "Behold I have graven thee upon the palms of my hands" (Isaiah 54: 16). The symbol that is other than myself and that is within me is one that I may hope to glimpse, if only fleetingly, in silence. It is a hidden theme out of which many of life's variations will arise. And yet in general no one can write about it, or even to think about it. It is other than "the brilliant darkness of a hidden silence" that Dionysius describes (in Luibheid, 1987: 135). What we think we know is like a river that leads to a domain of many subterranean rivers. There is no explanation.

Most created beings, Moses apart, are unable to tolerate the increate. The people will perish if they think to gaze on it (Exodus 19: 21). Moses survives in the darkness for 40 days and 40 nights "in a state beyond nature" (Gregory of Nyssa, in Malherbe & Ferguson, 1978: 46). The imagination and revelation present themselves as urgent and perennial facts in the eternal now. It is not so much that Moses plunges into darkness as that the darkness immerses him. It is not the darkness of grief. It is not the darkness associated with a state of increasing unknowing, as can occur when habitual modes of communication drift apart. The question of psychology or of psychopathology has no bearing. Moses is chosen in circumstances in which the meaning of being chosen is undefined.

Sufi insight offers a tantalising parallel. A young prince, who appears in the apocryphal Gospel according to Thomas, is struck by spiritual blindness on entering Egypt. He finds himself in a spiritual prison. He has lost the key to revelation.

The parents of the young prince send him from the east, his homeland, symbolized as the land of the Parthians, to the west, symbolized as Egypt, in order to attain the unique pearl (gnosis). The youth leaves the east, removes his robes of light, and arrives in in Egypt as a stranger. He wears the same garments as the Egyptians, so as not to be an object of suspicion. The food he is given erases his memory. He forgets that he is the son of a king. By way of a message from home, he remembers his royal origins and the nature of his quest. He makes away with the pearl and leaves behind his impure garments. When he arrives at the border he dresses again in the robes of light, which is one of the most beautiful gnostic symbols of the heavenly self.

[HENRY CORBIN, 1973: 159-160]

The interim between the increate and the created world of Genesis, like the interim between the Platonic One and the manifold, is where the symbol forms. It could be that the aim in life – if life is to have an aim – is to realise the meaning of a symbol that few if any of us may be aware of as other than an intuition of the unknowable. A presence looms out of a radiant fog. Someone perceives beneath the surface of the ocean the transient blur of a great fish. Appearances of this kind cannot be willed, and they cannot be pursued. Storms at sea and earthquakes intimate its powers. The void–light is a vision of ultimate destruction as well as of original creation. It is beyond the pale.

Silence terrified the mathematician and philosopher Blaise Pascal. *"Le silence est la plus grande persécution"*

(Pascal, 1670: 551). Silence may be terrifying because of a bad conscience, or terrifying because between it and the immeasurable void of Genesis there is no certain concept of distance. It is like travelling in Russell's balloon. "*Le silence éternel de ces espaces infinis m'effraie*" (ibid.: 256). In the theology of the Eastern Church, the silence of grace, as the silence of the Holy Spirit, or as the silence of the sacrifice, or as the silence of the Word, bear witness to the unknowable. Under the aegis of the unknowable, they are kin. No one can bear timeless origination, although it dwells in the self as a genius that no one is capable of tolerating. Some people seek for it in environments that are inhospitable, on the assumption that nature at its most desolate is associated with it. A poet, pondering in reverie on intimations of the symbol, may look, as did Coleridge, to a creationist paradigm and discover meaning in shapes that otherwise elude definition. It is dangerous: a theophany in the desert can point to extinction. Body, language and the type of edifice thought to be sacred are as one in a moment of disablement. Communication fails. There is a sense of nothing and nowhere. In my view, the darkness that Moses plunges into is a reflection in the created world of the void–light of the Genesis creation.

In the active life, I can measure silence negatively as an interruption. In the contemplative life, I am without measure. In the active life, the concept of experience is meaningful because I can suppose the existence of a subject and an object. In the silence of the sacrifice, the one object that exists must disappear and in this way must invalidate the idea of selfhood. Only with the ceasing of any exchange between subject and object does immanence as a way to transcendence take the place of experience. Immanence has a resonance that the concept of experience can never have. In contemplation, womb-like, mind enters a state of immanence so as to have access to transcendence. In a similar way, the young woman in Fra Filippo Lippi's "Annunciation" receives the silence of the sacrifice in the form of a child. In Christian prayer an incarnated god must die in order to be reborn as Pantocrator. In terms of the unconscious, an imaginary twin must die in order that I might be born. Such a loss is inseparable from the coming into being of a symbol that within itself enfolds the multiple means of expression that constitute life.

The silence that is intrinsic to the theme of beginnings, as well as to the theme of the sacrifice, gives rise to the symbol as a mystery within the womb and as a theophany that the disciplines of theology or psychotherapy cannot secure. H.-C. Puech (1938), in a remarkable essay, asked whether Dionysius had an experience of unknowing comparable to his description of the darkness that Moses entered. This speculation is of marginal importance so far as I am concerned. Whatever happened to Moses is beyond explanation, although Exodus presents what happened as a fact. And whatever happened to Dionysius is beyond understanding also. Immanence is other than experience, and the empiricist will disavow it and its companion, which is transcendence. The created world is isolated from its source in transcendence if it lacks the definitions of Coleridge and Lossky. Isolated from the increate, the created world exists on the verge of meaning. Experience without an allusion to immanence is bereft. The symbol in entering the created world gives expression to wonder.

The created world attempts to validate the claim that it is self-sufficient. It is unable to tolerate any return of the increate. A self-sufficient world is one that has no place for a transcendence that might enter it like a thunderbolt. If I read the books of Moses as history, then Hiebert's factual claim that the first Israelites were hill farmers is convincing. If I read them as giving expression to a topography of the imagination, in which the increate breaks into the created, then I find convincing the assertion that the Israelites were nomads who required the abstract nature of the wilderness as a necessary ground to theophany. The values attributed to nature recede in meaning if the increate should break into the created world. To read the books of Moses as history goes against the belief that the present is meaningful because it is a harbinger of a symbol that comes into being out of conditions that are not present in the created world.

In the created world, time and space are fictions that validate individuality. Each wave is real in its own way as it swells up and falls on the shore. It would appear that the increate has withdrawn from the created world, and that no one regrets this loss. Only if I enable the created world to return into the increate do I realise the expression of anguish. Imagine the demiurge of the *Timaeus* to restore time and the heavens to the eternal. Every wave would be one wave as time ceases. Moses enters a darkness in which time and space are unformed. There is no scope for prediction.

I open myself to silence and then, by a means of transition that I do not understand, I intuit an immeasurable that seems to be a vague presence, without force, and yet that draws me towards it. Dissatisfied by this approach, I attempt to reverse the situation and to begin with the immeasurable as the source to silence. In this way, I enter into certain Hellenic and Judeo–Christian traditions of thought that are alien to me and yet strangely welcoming. The immeasurable is the infinite. Some people have a passion for the infinite while others do not, and between the two there is no agreement.

The immeasurable and the infinite in common elude the grasp of thought. J. B. Haldane, the biologist, is alleged to have claimed that "the universe is not only queerer than we suppose, but queerer that we can suppose". A universe grounded in the infinite is certainly queer; it is like a house built on shifting sands. On occasion, the infinite is deified or demonized. Attempts to explain it by reason are as alien to it as are the attempts ritually to propitiate it by means of acts of sacrifice. In psychoanalytic conjecture, the source of mind lies with the unconscious presence of the combined object. Thinkers of an earlier time understood the unconscious (which they did not fully articulate) as originating mind in the infinite. In the thought of Parmenides, Plato, of Plotinus and of others, the infinite signifies the One. Does the combined object carry the significance of the One or the infinite? Comparisons of this kind are always suspect, and yet the combined object and the One appear to be approximates in E. R. Dodds' description of the One in Plotinus as overflowing with life.

> For Plotinus all Being derives from the overspill of a single infinite reservoir of force, a reservoir which is, in Blake's language, not a cistern but a fountain. (cf. Plotinus 6.5.12.5) And this initial dynamism communicates itself to all the subsequent levels of existence. The Platonic Forms are no mere static archetypes, as Aristotle mistakenly supposed (Met. 991b4); creative potency is the very stuff of their being (6.4.9). And the overspill continues in the sensible world. Nature, in Plotinus' homely metaphor, "boils over with life" (6.5.12.9); and life is at all levels a transmission of power. . . . For Plotinus the universe had no origin; there was never a time when the fountain did not

overflow, just as there will never be a time when it runs dry. Causation is not an event; it is a relationship of timeless dependence by which the intelligible world is sustained in eternal being.

[DODDS, 1960: 3]

If it were to speak, the infinite might say that without its presence there would be no generation of mind. The created world, if it could be personified, would deny this claim. It has no place for the infinite within the ideas of process and development that characterise it. The infinite, if it enters the created world, of necessity generates pain. I have no notion of how the infinite brings into existence the mind of the foetus, although according to my understanding it is a moment that each of us must have passed through. Only by way of the imagination can I approach this moment. William Golding began his novel *Darkness Visible* with a vision of a great ball of fire that gathers itself together out of the conflagration of the London Blitz. A small child steps out of a huge ball of fire and walks towards the reader. I take Golding's vision as a metaphor for mind's origination by means of the infinite. The fire of originality is an intense white light that radiates through the mist out of which mind forms. Some of the early Romantic poets sought to apply a metaphysical insight to foetal psychology, as did William Wordsworth in his "Intimations of Immortality": "Our birth is but a sleep and forgetting; / The soul that rises with us, our life's star, / Hath had elsewhere its setting, / And cometh from afar. Not in entire forgetfulness, / And not in utter nakedness, / But trailing clouds of glory do we come.

. . ." A parent may look on the face of a newborn child and transiently think to see there an unworldly depth of wisdom.

Plotinus is able to bring together the infinite, in the form of the unknowable One, with the good (my understanding of the benevolence of silence) and with beauty. The good, Plotinus believes, is always present, even in sleep. It is a still small voice that must be attended to carefully if it is to be heard. It is always gentle. Beauty, on the other hand, is associated with a mental pain that is often intense, even though it and the good derive from the same source, which is the One. Without referring to the unconscious, Plotinus is fully aware of its import in psychology. He writes about what we may have forgotten and yet may long for. A corollary of this theme is his concern with that which we are unable to remember and yet cannot be freed from, a residual pain that is inherent in mental origination. The residual pain is reflected in any experience of beauty in daily life.

> The apprehension of that which is beautiful is there already for those who in their way know it and have awakened to it, and so, too, the amazement, the awakening of love. But the good, since it was present of old as an innate desire, and is also present to those who are asleep, does not amaze those who sometimes see it, because it is always with them and there is never any recollection of it. People do not see it because it is present when they are asleep. But the love of that which is beautiful, when it is present, gives pain, because one must desire it having seen it. This love is secondary, and the fact that lovers are conscious of

it at once reveals the beauty to be secondary. But the desire, which is more ancient than this, and imperceptible, declares the Good to be more ancient and prior. . . . The good is gentle, pleasant and most delicate, and present to someone just when they wish it. But that which is beautiful brings amazement, shock and pain mixed with pleasure.

[ENNEAD V 5.12, IN GERSON, 2013: 48–49][1]

Rilke in the *Duino Elegies* describes beauty as terrifying. But the effect of beauty is other than the effect of terror. Fundamental to the quickening of life is the pain of a beauty that marks the entry of the ineffable into the created world. Any organism in coming to life must know this pain. The radiance of time as it emerges from the infinite is painful in its own way. In the narrative of the Annunciation, which I see as inseparable from the Genesis creation narrative, a young woman must know anguish as well as joy at bearing within her an emissary of the increate, who must of necessity in time enact the cataclysm of beauty through a terrible dying.

Essentially the good and the beautiful are not objects of knowledge, although out of them can arise the knowable. Their source lies elsewhere. In psychoanalytic thinking, the observer of the infant may delight in the infant's intimacy

[1] "One of the most celebrated theses of Plotinus is that the Beautiful and the Good are not the same. In the earliest of treatises we are told to cast off earthly pleasure and to seek the Beautiful; but it is also hinted, clearly though succinctly, that the Good, our final object, lies beyond: "And that which is beyond this we call the nature of the Good, and it has the Beautiful set before it" (*Ennead I* 6.9). At *Ennead V* 5.12, the Beautiful is not merely an inferior good, but it is also a shock, a danger and a distraction to the philosophic eye: "It entails amazement and shock, and mingles pleasure with that which causes pain; the unwary it drags away from the Good" (Edwards, 1991: 161–162).

with the nipple and the breast without recognising the unconscious significance of this experience. As part-object agents of the unconscious, the nipple and the breast are founded in the infinite and to a type of beginning, as mysterious in origin as the good and the beautiful are in the thought of Plotinus, or as are the Holy Spirit and the Word in the triadic thinking of the Gospels.

Franz Kafka has a parable in his short story, The Great Wall of China, in which a messenger brings a final message from the dying emperor to you, the reader. It is in the nature of the message that the messenger, in bringing the message, must undergo a breakdown in which time and space lose direction. There is no evidence that the message will reach its destination, since the messenger is disabled by the charisma of the message. And yet one evening the message reaches you out of the air as you sit quietly on your veranda. The poetic effect of this conclusion lies in the fact that Kafka does not explain how, in spite of the disabling of every means of communication, the message should have reached you. The infinite is implicit in this disjunction. It is the source of poetic resonance. What had seemed so remote when thought of as the immeasurable, now asserts itself by way of an absence that has a phantom-like presence. The One is implicit rather than explicit in the triad that it constitutes with the good and the beautiful. In the evolving model of the Gospels known as the Trinity, the Father (as the unknowable infinite) and the Son (as the agent for a revelation that is cataclysmic) and the Holy Spirit (as typifying the grace of silence) are able to operate together, on condition that on entry into the created world one of the three will be imperceptible, no reason being given for this condition. The breakdown of the messenger in Kafka's parable signifies (for me) the cataclysm of revelation, which is the suffering implicit in the act of being incarnated. There is no way of singing or speaking the infinite: only by way of opening the mind to silence, and by disavowing selfhood, can the presence of the infinite be sensed by means of the immeasurable.

The existence of the infinite in Kafka's parable, in spite of its suspension – a suspension that in fact increases the intensity of the infinite – is a key to Kafka's writings in general, in the form of a vastness so great that anyone who attempts to cross it on horseback will disappear. "Our land is so vast that no fairy tale can give an inkling of its size. The heavens can scarcely span it" (in Pasley, 1973: 71). The vastness is similar to the effect of a star that died millennia ago and whose light is now about to reach the earth. The immeasurable on this point loses any relation that it might have to measure. Revelation, as the increate entering the created world, carries within it its own negation. The infinite is seldom an encouraging presence in Kafka's writings. No divine edict is needed to destroy everything if the infinite as a negative form of revelation is present. Walls crumble. No one ever completes a project, let alone completes a project on time. The impalpable effect of the infinite is like a father who offers up his child to sacrifice. In this context, any entering of the increate into the created world will reveal itself as persistent fatigue and sense of futility, as in the building of the Great Wall of China, or the building of the tower at Babel, with which Kafka compares the construction of the Great Wall. There is more than a touch of Bruegel's insight in Kafka's perception. I now see that the silence that I experienced when contemplating the Bruegel "Tower of Babel" in Rotterdam depended on the presence within silence of an infinite that endorses the majesty of this extraordinary construction, as well as undermines the enterprise of those who are attempting to construct it. The infinite equally says and unsays. The tower fascinates Bruegel too much to be thought of as an error. It is an enigma against which the infinite presses. Anyone who thinks to generate form must know this pressure.

The disabling power of the infinite shows itself in states of confinement as well as in open spaces. People enjoy festivities in one part of a Bruegel painting, and no one notices that to one side, in a corner, Christ is being crucified. Similarly in Kafka's tale, the people who jostle in the narrow streets of the capital are unaware that in a square close to them the emperor is about to be executed. If I acknowledge the existence of the infinite, I may come to think that an inability to arrest the cruel compulsion to destroy the joy of others accounts in part for the bereft state of the created world.

It is in the nature of Kafka's sense of the vast that the gaps between the built sections of the Great Wall of China seem to increase. Parts that should be connected give more and more evidence of being separated, the gaps widening as the vast seeps in. The Genesis account of the building of the tower conveys the insight that between the building of the tower and the formation and the deformation of languages there is a connection. The infinite determines both the formation and the deformation by means of a symbolisation that the conscious mind has no knowledge of. The Great Wall and the Tower are constructs of this kind. They enable other symbols to form. They are defences against the "barbarians", whoever they may be.[1] The belief that they are failed as enterprises does not override the observation that both of them have fascinated artists through the ages. Although you cannot measure the infinite, you can create a fiction in stone that appears to intimate the infinite as an idea.

Opening oneself to silence is the first stage in a process of discovering intuitions that differ from the intuitions that are instruments of thought. There is a diminishing of any sense of subject and with it a diminishing of any sense of object. And yet the immeasurable and the infinite influence experience in ways that experience cannot understand. Means of demarcation disappear in the steady contemplative gaze. Spatial and temporal points of reference no longer exist. Plotinus believed that mind had to be everywhere if the concept of mind was to be meaningful. If the outside is inside, then the inside is everywhere. If I see silence and the infinite join with cataclysm as parts of a triad, then opening myself to silence is clearly an activity that entails a fundamental re-organisation of personality. Nothing is easy in the interim that lies between having an experience of silence and the infinite.

---

[1] It is thought that the texts of the Veda are impervious to the effect of the infinite. At no time do they deteriorate or disappear.

There exists in Byzantium a strong and well represented
tradition . . . that views the incarnation of the Word as the
fundamental mystery of creation, conceived of by God before
all eternity.

[BUCUR, 2008: 200]

In the Rabbinic exegesis of Genesis 1: 1–3 it was maintained
that before God spoke there was silence. Certainly such
a picture would appeal to the Hellenistic world where, as
we know, from the magical papyri and from the hymns to
"silence", that silence was the mark of the deus absconditus.
A quasi-personification of the divine word in Wisdom 18: 14
has God's almighty word leap down from the heaven "when
silence encircled all things". Ignatius of Antioch, who seems to
offer an early echo of Johannine thought, speaks of God whose
'word proceeded from silence'. He puts a similar stress on the
Incarnation as wrought in silence.

[BROWN, 1966: 524]

Lossky's concept of revelation postulates the existence of
a gap between the Genesis act of creation and the world
created by the act. Without revelation, the inhabitants of
the created world will have no access to the act by which
they were created. The imagination according to Coleridge performs a similar function: it reveals what otherwise
would not be revealed. Neither definition allows for the
possibility that the fundamental meaning of creation existed
before the act of creation and that this meaning eludes any
attempt to define it in terms of time. According to this view,
"the fundamental mystery of creation conceived of by God

before all eternity" (Bucur, 2008: 200) is the Incarnation, or the Word made Flesh. It is in the nature of the immeasurable that although it is always present, it cannot be grasped by thought. The Word made Flesh presents itself as both idea and actuality. It is of the immeasurable as the unthinkable at its most acute. It transforms the meaning of the Genesis act of creation. In effect, the phrase "In the beginning was the Word", which opens the Gospel of St John, has to operate on a different and unascertainable plane from "In the beginning God created the heavens and the earth."[1] The Word made Flesh is both unthinkable and intolerable, being intolerable because unthinkable, and having no reflection in mind or in the natural world. (I may think to have a picture in my imagination of the Genesis creation narrative, and artists have attempted to depict it. I am unable to have a picture in my imagination of the Word made Flesh.)

No one can tolerate the meaning of the Word made Flesh, which takes the unique form of Christ. Anywhere, and among any group, He must be extirpated. "He came unto his own, and his own received him not" (John 1: 11). In this form, the truth of revelation arouses outrage and the desire to kill or be killed. So Jesus speaks: "By now ye seek to kill me, a man that hath told you the truth, which I heard from God: this did not Abraham" John 8: 40).

The idea of a reality that is prior to the Genesis creation narrative has an earlier precedence. Revelation appears

[1] "A rabbinical commentary describes the existence of seven things before the world was created as the Torah, Repentance, Paradise, Gehenna, the Throne of Glory, the Sanctuary and the name of the Messiah" (Dodd, 1953: 85).

before any act of creation as Wisdom in the books of Moses. As Wisdom herself proclaims, "Yahweh created me at the beginning of his work, the first of his acts of old. Ages ago I was set up, at the first, before the beginning of the earth" (Proverbs 8).

> The Lord possessed me in the beginning of his way, before his works of old. I was set up from everlasting, from the beginning, or ever the world was. When there were no depths, when there were no fountains abounding with water, before the mountains were settled, before the hills I was brought forth. While as yet he had not made the earth, or the fields, or the highest part of the dust of the world. I was there when he prepared the heavens or when he set the compass on the face of the depth, when he established the clouds above, and when he strengthened the fountains of the deep.
>
> [PROVERBS 9: 1–28]

Wisdom is inaccessible, and yet she is present everywhere.

> Man puts his hand to the flinty rock and overturns mountains by the roots. He cuts out channels in the rocks, and his eye sees every precious thing. He stops up streams so that they do not trickle, and the thing that is hid he brings forth to light. But where shall wisdom be found? And where is the place of understanding?
>
> [JOB, 28]

Wisdom is to be found somewhere in the world; it is there, but it is incapable of being grasped. If it were not inside the world, the reference (in Job, 28) to men digging through the earth would be meaningless. On the other hand – and this admittedly is remarkable – it is separated from the works of creation. This "wisdom", this "understanding" must signify something like the "meaning" implanted by God in creation, the divine something of creation. . . . Wisdom, the order given to the world by God, is the most precious thing of all. But while man has found a way to all precious things, he does not find his way to the mystery of creation. Only God knows its place, for He has already been concerned with it at creation. Man cannot determine this mystery of creation; it is out of his reach. He never gets it into his power as he does other precious things. The world never reveals the mystery of its order.

[VON RAD, 1970: 148]

It is unclear whether Wisdom is a little girl born from the mouth of the God or whether (in a more literal interpretation) She is the Word that God speaks in order to initiate creation. Genesis 2: 6 has a mist rise from the earth and water the face of the earth. The birth of Wisdom is similar. "I came out of the mouth of the most High and covered the earth as a cloud" (Sirach 24: 3). She is the beloved, the daughter as well as the wife of the Creator. "Then I was by Him, as a nursling; And I was daily all delight, playing always before Him (Proverbs 8: 30).[2] A commentator recalls the time of the

[2] Compare Heraclitus, Fragment 94. "Lifetime is a child at play, moving pieces in a game. Kingship belongs to the child."

marriage of Wisdom to the Creator. "She comes towards him like a mother and receives him like a young wife" (Ecclesiasticus 15.2). However, she is not heeded, in spite of the fact that she cries out from the heights or from "beside the gates at the entrance to the town" (Proverbs 8).

"Wisdom hath built her house, she hath hewn out her seven pillars. . . . She crieth upon the highest places of the city, 'Who so is simple, let him turn in hither'. As for him that wanteth understanding, she saith to him, 'Come eat of my bread and drink of the wine that I have mingled'" (Proverbs 9: 1–5). The theologians of Byzantine Russia ascribed a dual meaning to this text. Churches of the Orthodox Faith were identified with the house that Wisdom built, and they were often named Sophia, meaning wisdom (Haghia Sofia in Istanbul being an example). They frequently carried pictures of the seven pillars. And in the ceremony of the Eucharist, they translated Wisdom's offering of bread and wine into the bread and wine of the embodied Logos. The church was identified with Sophia as the Virgin Mother, who carries within her (or on Her lap) the living Christ as the Incarnation. In this way Wisdom and the Incarnation are united before the beginning of any beginning as mother and child. The light of the Annunciation shines through the transparency of the Genesis creation narrative and encloses every nursing couple. Some commentators in Byzantine Russia doubted whether the Mother or the Son should carry the title of Wisdom. Archbishop Gennady of Novgorod (in office from 1484 to 1504) was so perturbed by the identification of Wisdom with the person of the Virgin that he "considered it necessary to re-assert vigorously the identification of Wisdom with the hypostatic Logos, Second Person of the Trinity" (Meyendorff, 1987: 400). In Trinitarian thought, the Wisdom of the mother, which is the Wisdom of the Holy Spirit, co-exists in harmony with the Wisdom of the Son, which is the wisdom of the Word.

> Behind the Logos doctrine lies a more Jewish and less metaphysical Sophia doctrine. An early Christian teaching about Jesus proclaimed him as the Wisdom of God.
>
> [RENDEL HARRIS, 1917: 57]

> Jesus is identified with the Wisdom of God and the Word of God successively: first with Wisdom because the Logos doctrine is originally a Wisdom doctrine, and after that with the Word because Wisdom becomes the Word.
>
> [IBID.: 12]

Our point of departure is the Book of Proverbs, especially the eighth chapter, with an occasional divergence into the Psalms. Genesis comes later in the argument. When we explain "Let us make man", Wisdom is introduced, already identified with the Creative Instrument from Proverbs. This Wisdom is either the Divine Conjugate or the divine Offspring; it is not clear which. If she is the former, then the Logos is her son. If she is the latter, then the Logos is her brother. The former position leads on to the curious Word of Christ in the Gospel of Hebrews, "My Mother the holy Ghost", the latter to the twinship of Jesus and the Holy Spirit, as we find it in the *Pistis Sophia*.

[IBID.: 48]

Abraham Heschel has remarkably defined how the group may experience the onset of a new idea that is not evident in the creation of the created world. "The prophet is human and yet he employs notes on an octave too high for our ideas. He experiences moments that defy our understanding. He is neither 'a singing saint' nor a moralising poet, but an assaulter of mind. Often his words begin to burn where conscious ends" (Heschel, 1962: 12). The notion that words begin to burn at the point where consciousness as well as conscience ends is astonishing. Spiritual insight when no definition is able to contain it can induce mental dullness, not least among the intelligent. Imagine a novel – I am thinking of Dostoevsky – in which the plot forms out of the unpredictable psychic energies that activate the genius of the author. The author is possessed by a new yet still unarticulated idea – which in fact is the oldest of ideas – and has entered the throes of a birth process so threatening that it may have to be terminated. Many of the characters that this author writes about are immersed in states of incoherence. Fearfully they intimate the existence of "a before" that is before any beginning and that underpins creation in ways that created beings are unable to understand. In this experience, an eruption of that which is before any beginning can present itself as a revelation, whose effects operate beyond the limits of understanding. The new idea cannot be controlled. It threatens the complacence that in the created world can masquerade as sanity. The group under assault may think of itself as tricked.

> In the beginning was the Word, and the Word was with God, and the Word was God. The same was in the beginning with God. All things were made by him; and without him was not anything made that was made. In him was life; and the life was the light of men. And the light shineth in darkness; and the darkness comprehended it not.
>
> [JOHN 1: 1–5]

Poetry at its most sublime, as in this case, can represent truths that are not of this world and that enter the world like a thunderbolt. There is a reaching-out in early philosophy to understand this type of insight. Heraclitus (fragment 119) writes about the thunderbolt as an otherworldly amalgam of thunder and lightning that pilots or steers everything; it as an analogue for Zeus's death-dealing spear, and it intimates the visionary Word. Hippolytus, in a commentary (Kahn, 1979: 271), claimed that the thunderbolt of Heraclitus signifies an eternal fire that is intelligent and can organise the universe as a "need and satiety". The "need" is a need to construct a world order. The "satiety", conversely, is a conflagration that will bring the world to an end. Like Wisdom, or the ancient Egyptian Ma'at, the insight is of a cosmic "justice" that informs experience and to which experience cannot have access. In Plato's dialogue, *Cratylus*, Socrates recalls a conversation about the nature of justice:

I persist in asking what he takes justice to be, and he says fire. But this is not easy to understand. Another says it is not fire itself but the very heat that fire represents. Another laughs at these views and says that justice is what Anaxagoras meant: intelligence (*nous*). It is the supreme power and, being mixed with nothing else, it sets all things in order *by moving through them.*

[PLATO, *CRATYLUS*, 413B3–C7]

Among Stoic philosophers, Logos was a divine physical energy that permeated reality in the form of a fiery ether (Hägg, 2006: 182).

Logos, the star-born tongue: how came
So stark a statement from a scroll,
Consumed, as though the dead could tame
All moods by midnight's strict control?
Fire in a moment flies intent
The works of reason to unwind.
How to reconcile that element
To the slow writing of mankind?

[VERNON WATKINS, "LOGOS"]

Heschel's prophet assaults mind by way of a revelation that the human mind cannot tolerate. He stirs emotions that disable understanding. The prophet's words "begin to burn where conscious ends". In the case of Christ, the effect is of a pronouncement embodied. Christ is not a prophet, and He bears no truth. He is the truth, an antithesis to the metaphoric and the figurative. He is the sacrifice, the message as well as the bearer of the message. The effect of contracting the message into the figure of the messenger is painful beyond bearing. Individuals observing the gentleness, the humility and the insight of Christ were overwhelmed. The group could not stand Him. He was like a scream that everyone registers, even though no one can hear the scream. It could have happened with any group. In this case, it happened to be a Jewish community – I think chosen because of a Jewish hypersensitivity to the spiritual. Apart from Pilate and the soldiers who carry out the torture and death sentence, everyone in the Gospel of St John is Jewish, including St John himself. Christ and the disciples are Jewish, and so are the people who feel offended by such assertions as "Before Abraham was I am" (John 8: 58). There is a sense in which the group was scapegoated as well as violated. From the opening pages of the Gospel of St John, people cry out for Christ to be stoned. It is a desolating and grim fact that over the centuries many Christians and other non-Jews have used the claim of "the Jews" as crying for the death of Christ as a pretext for a virulent anti-Semitism. There is a failure to understand that it is in the nature of Revelation that it is scandalous. Any interpretation of it must waver without resolution between a symbolic and a literalist type of thinking. There is no way of keeping a focus. The meaning of the Russian icon lies not in the icon's relation with the spectator; it lies in the icon's relation to the Mystery that it portrays. In Revelation, however, there is no differentiation between the icon and the Mystery. Within the blinding light of Revelation, no icon can be seen. Silence, as the Holy Spirit working in conjunction with the Son, opens out the space of the imagination in the direction of the immeasurable, or contracts this space to a point that invalidates the imagination. Revelation and the imagination are no longer companions: this is a result of there being a beginning before the beginning. "I am the Light of the World. Whoever follows me will not walk in darkness but will have the light of life" (John: 8: 12). That is it: everything or nothing. All the evidence and achievements of the human mind are as dust. The Gospel of St John, as an example of the greatest poetry, communicates a sense of otherness that challenges everything that the reader knows and feels.

A mark of the greatest poetry is that no act of appropriation can claim it. The unresolved literalism is disquieting. Are the bread and wine of the Eucharist symbols of Christ's sacrifice, or have they been transmuted into His flesh and blood? Insights of this kind stir the heart in part because of their irresolution. In one miracle or "sign", Christ spits into a piece of clay and then kneads the clay so that he can place it on the eyes of a blind man (John 9: 6). An Incarnation that precedes the act of creation is able to divinise all evidence of matter. It can transform clay into a substance that restores sight. The Revelation of the Gospel of St John is not imaginative; it is not conducive to reverie or dream. It touches on other springs. It is an eruption of types of unconscious thought that are seldom acknowledged.

Rudolf Bultmann has made this point in a way that I find remarkable. His insights illuminate the text in ways that I cannot relate to my life and yet in disturbing me surely do relate to my life. They are thoughts that "begin to burn where

conscious ends". He proposes that "The only way of present-
ing revelation is as the annihilating of everything human,
the refusal of all human qualities, the rejection of all human
answers – in short, as putting man into question" (Bultmann,
in Ashton, 1991: 58). In a closely argued commentary on the
Gospel of St John, Bultmann has claimed that each of us has
an innate – and misleading – knowledge of revelation, which
is "a knowledge of one's own situation that leads one to seek
constantly for its true meaning". Knowledge of this kind can
lead to self-destruction if anyone attempts to derive from it
"the criteria of God's judgment and the reality of Revelation"
(Bultmann, 1964: 61–62).

> For it only becomes reality as an event that passes
> all understanding. Our prior knowledge is nega-
> tive knowledge: the knowledge of human limitation
> with its estrangement from God, combined with
> the knowledge that human mind must look to God
> for its salvation: the knowledge that God does not
> confront me in my world, and yet he must confront
> me if my life is to be a true life. . . . The decisive ques-
> tion is therefore whether man, when confronted by
> the event of the Revelation, will remain true to his
> genuine prior knowledge of the Revelation, whereby
> he sees it as an other-worldly event which passes
> judgment on him and his world; or whether he will
> make his own illusory ideas the criterion by which to
> judge it; that is, whether he will choose to judge Reve-
> lation only by these worldly standards and values. *The
> event of Revelation is a question and an offence* [italics
> added]. . . . Human beings expect that the Revelation

will somehow give proof of itself and that it will be in some way recognisable. For them the One who reveals – although of course he must appear in a human form – must in some way appear as a shining mysterious figure, as a hero or miracle worker or mystagogue. His humanity must be no more than a disguise; it must be transparent. . . . All such desires are cut short by the statement that the Word became Flesh. It is in his sheer humanity that he is the One who reveals.

[BULTMANN, 1964: 63–64]

The identification of the Word and Flesh is based on a contradiction, which is concrete in its literalism as well as multiple in its symbolism. Nothing in the created world prepares created beings for this truth. The puzzle is this: it is not innate and yet it is prior to all creation. It makes a fool of the succession known as time. The Messenger, like the messenger in Kafka's parable, invalidates natural process. He goes against the grain of the sequential. In place of birth, life and death, He proposes the different order of death as a threshold into a rebirth, whose life the imagination cannot comprehend. The linearity of the Flesh as existing in time is lost within an idea of surcease that is self-transfiguring rather than entropic.[3]

---

[3] Coleridge does not see the imaginative in the Word made Flesh. In my view, he avoids making this relation, which might draw attention to the limitations of the imaginative. As Bultmann has indicated, the actuality of the Word made Flesh has no source in mind or nature. It has no connection with imaginative endowment. The fact that it occurred once, and once only, increases the prospect of failure in any attempt to relate it to the deposit of human inheritance.

The mind in contemplation is barely grounded in immanence and travels towards transcendence as silence enters it. I might think of a mother as lifting her child to the breast, or to some other means of nourishment, and the child as intuiting an oceanic significance to the interior of the feeding object that is synonymous with intuitions that it might have concerning the mysterious and generative interior of the womb. The silence that the contemplative mind opens itself to cannot be measured. The steeds of Parmenides, rising into the heavens, have already removed thought from its habitual relation to time and space. Silence is the ground to creativity. I would have no intuition concerning the meaning of its grace, if I had no idea of the Holy Spirit. But once I think of the Holy

Spirit, I find myself drawn into the alien and awesome logic of a triune mystery. In the language of psychoanalysis, one witness to the immeasurable is the feeding mother, which on the concrete level of unconscious thinking is the breast, and another witness is the imaginary child within the breast that, as the Redeemer of the world, illuminates the one who feeds at the breast. In theological terms, the flow of the breast signifies the grace of the Holy Spirit, while the imaginary twin in the breast embodies the beauty and cataclysm of revelation, sometimes known as the sacrifice.

Contemplative silence veils the presence of the Son within itself, as much as it indicates by grace the presence of the Holy Spirit. I start from transcendental conjecture and see where it leads me. It is a leap into the extraordinary: and yet it must be so, if silence is to show an otherness within itself, which is a disturbance that refutes the laws of the natural world. The presence of the Incarnation is primordial. It enters time and space once, and once only. A majestic drama is enacted in dimensions to which I have no access.

The Genesis creation narrative entails acts of making in time. It is evidential, and its evidence can be sullied and even destroyed. But the co-existence of the Word and Flesh involves no act of making. It disables any natural conception of time and space. It cannot be sullied. The stuff of life is conceived of differently in either case. I look on the natural world with awe and see the narratives of creation as paradigms that give expression to wonder by way of the imagination. But the revelation of the Word made Flesh does not invite the imaginative to enter into this world. It disarms the poetry of nature and denies validity to history, even before anyone has thought to define the discipline of history. It challenges and undermines the significance of creation as act and consequence. It subverts the distinction of *natura naturans* or *natura naturata*. By means of two witnesses, a mother and child, the immeasurable is able to destroy or create symbolisation.

Melanie Klein proposed that it was possible to regain a past that has never been lost, even though it has been forgotten, by means of "memory in feeling". Opening myself to silence, I find that a power within me has me review my life. Once more I am an infant taking its first breath or feeding at the source of being as though this were the first pulse. But the recall has a greater significance. Memories in feeling can be without visual or aural reference. They may override the concept of the past or escape from the values of history. In effect, they may be intuitions of an eternal that cannot be thought. Erroneously, memory in feeling can be confused with a type of *recherche du temps perdu* in which a recall of the past confines the individual to a certain history and denies any validity to the eternal, even though the resonance of this return depends on a claim to endorse the oceanic. Using memory, or any other means of holding on, destroys the experience. There has to be a letting go.

The theologian Panayiotis Nellas has claimed that "man is an indissoluble psychosomatic unity with unfathomable psychic depths" (Nellas, 1987: 27). In terms of immanence, the connection between the unfathomable psychic depths and the indissoluble psychosomatic unity is contingent. The unfathomable psychic depths are no more than an append-age to the indissoluble psychosomatic unity. In terms of transcendence, the unfathomable psychic depths are indis-solubly related to the psychosomatic unity. It is why the psychosomatic unity exists.

In the first of his *Meditations*, René Descartes attempts (and has the courage to fail) to reach transcendence by means of reason. In order to release himself from falsehood, Descartes asserts he must remove the mental rubbish of a lifetime by practising a radical scepticism. He advises the reader to carry out a similar therapy at least once in a lifetime.

> Some years ago I was struck by the large number of falsehoods that I had accepted as true in my child-hood, and by the highly doubtful nature of the whole edifice that I had subsequently based on them. I real-ised that it was necessary, once in the course of my life, to demolish everything completely and to start right again from the foundations if I wanted to estab-lish anything at all in the sciences that was stable and likely to last.
>
> [DESCARTES, IN COTTINGHAM, STOOTHOFF, & MURDOCH, 1984: 12]

He summons up a malign demon to question him at every turn concerning any assumption that his common sense might rely on. He does not abandon his view that reason will sustain his belief in the meaningful nature of the concept of certainty. His resort to the malign demon is intended to free him from the charms of fable or the phantoms of mental disorder. His fear of madness is genuinely real. But his attempt to prove the existence of God by means of reason is bound to fail. It is not possible to reach transcendence by this means. Descartes is unable to separate a certain idea of science from an idea of the infallible. He seems to think of the scientist simply as a being that reasons. Isaac Newton is still to be born, and Descartes has no one to challenge his assumption that genius in science does not entail a dabbling in the occult. He traps thought within the confines of a certain conception of identity. The malign demon is predictable. He is *ordinary*. His questioning does not entail the illogical. It does not leap from one dimension to another to escape from immanence. It is not Zen.

The imaginary twin, whether as the malign demon or as the incarnated Son, is inseparable from the trauma of conversion. It says: you are dead and I am alive, and only by acknowledging the fact of your spiritual death will you have a glimmer of truth. Two African narratives reveal how the move into transcendence can go wrong and how the imaginary twin can take on an occult quality that is more nightmarish than Descartes' malign demon. The narratives centre on the umbilical cord and the placenta, rather than on the imaginary twin and the breast. At one time, the people of Baganda (now part of Uganda) believed that the placenta when discarded at the time of the king's birth was the king's dreaded twin. In ritual, the stump of the umbilical cord was thought to represent the twin, while the placenta represented a mother identified with the moon. The imaginary twin puts the king's life at risk if there are no acts of propitiation associated with the sight of a full moon. The Egyptologist A. M.

Blackman (1916) has drawn a parallel between this belief and a myth derived from neighbouring Egypt concerning the nature of the moon god Khons, who is a prince without any defining characteristics, apart from his compelling physical charm and his ability to absorb into himself the good qualities of anyone who comes near him. In the mythology of Baganda, the severed umbilical cord of the king is similarly a destructive presence if it is not venerated: the stump, which is all that remains of the umbilical cord, is identified with a vengeful dead twin and – here is the parallel with Khons as a moon god – it is associated with dangerous powers of the moon.

> Once a month the Kimbugwe (the second officer of state) carried the "twin" into the royal presence and placed it before the king who took it out of its wrappings of bark cloth and after inspecting it returned it to the Kimbugwe, who wrapped it up and restored it to the temple. This was done at the time of the new moon. After the royal ceremony, the "twin" was exposed to the moon in the doorway of the temple. It was anointed with butter.
>
> [BLACKMAN, 1916: 249]

The moon–placenta is a version of the breast–womb that invests the imaginary twin, who in this case is Khons or the umbilical stump. The moon–mother enables Khons to absorb the personality of others and to endow the umbilical stump with the powers of magic. The imaginary twin and the breast, which in this case have the form of the placenta and umbilical cord, are phantoms with the power to disable the living couple.

... groping in a half-light where some may see a little further than others but where none sees beyond a certain point, and, like pilots in a mist, must rely upon a general sense of where they are and how to navigate in such weather and in such waters, with such help as they may derive from maps drawn at other dates by men employing different conventions, and by the aid of such instruments as give nothing but the most general information about their situation.

[ISAIAH BERLIN, 1996: 37, WRITING ABOUT "A SENSE OF REALITY"]

At one stage in its formation, a certain type of symbol can present itself as cryptic. Ishmael, the narrator of Herman Melville's novel *Moby Dick*, finds himself looking at a painting whose configuration he cannot understand. It is cryptic in an unusual way: if it were decoded, it would show itself to be a symbol in formation.

> A very large oil painting so thoroughly be-smoked, and in every way defaced, that in the unequal cross-lights by which you viewed it, was only by diligent study and a series of systematic visits to it, and a careful enquiry of the neighbours, that you could in any way arrive at an understanding of its purpose. Such unaccountable masses of shades and shadows

that at first you almost thought some ambitious young artist, at the time of the New England hags, had endeavoured to delineate chaos bewitched. . . . What most puzzled and confounded you was a long, limber, portentous black mass of something hovering in the centre of the picture. . . . There was a sort of indefinite, half-attained, unimaginable sublimity about it that fairly froze you to it. . . . Does it not bear a faint resemblance to a gigantic fish? Even the great leviathan himself?

[MELVILLE, 1851: 25]

The issue of talent does not account for the fascination that the painting has for Ishmael. In a similar way, I might imagine that out of a chaotic state of notes and manuscripts the idea of the white whale called Moby Dick emerges as the symbol that enables Melville to realise his tale. An impulse towards integration is inherent in a fragmented state: the white whale is glimpsed everywhere in the painting without being clearly formed. Melville describes many attempts to paint the white whale, and he praises the French painter Garney for his attempts to depict it, but eventually he comes to the view that no artist can do it justice (Melville, 1851: 235). It is an existential truth that can be known intuitively and that cannot be truthfully depicted. Even to gain an idea of the whale's contour, the spectator needs to put life at risk by taking to the sea.[1] The incoherence of the painting signifies the forming of a potency out of the ocean in which it dwells. Like the Leviathan of the Psalms, which the psalmist thinks in error that

[1] A god that is not an existential presence is liable to be seized on as an idol.

he can slay, the white whale personifies the formless infinite. The hubris of Ahab, as captain of the *Pequod*, is to think that he can subdue this agent of the immeasurable. The symbol in opening out is vast beyond any conceivable vastness.

The wilderness shapes those who dwell in it. The hints of a white whale in the painting are inseparable from a theophany that forms out of the ocean and that in a series of lunges destroys the whaling-vessel *Pequod*. It would appear that the ocean as the wilderness – and by wilderness I understand a site of metaphysical or theological dimension – is able to concentrate itself into a great force that again and again assaults the whaling-vessel. Everybody on board must experience death. Ishmael alone escapes by means of floating on top of an empty coffin. It is in the nature of the symbol that it can return to the cryptic as well as be formed out of the cryptic; and in its being reformed its meanings may return to the unintelligible. The wooden surface of the coffin has carved markings on it in a language that Ishmael is unable to understand.

The demiurge's drawing of time and space out of the One is a prototype for this theory of the symbol. The radiance of the One shines through every strangeness like a light in a fog. Melville's protagonist, Ishmael, becomes friends with the "savage" and even barbaric Pacific Islander Queequeg in an intimacy that never loses its relation to the strange. At first, Ishmael is suspicious and even fearful of Queequeg, whose appearance and manner he finds fascinating as well disturbing. He spies on Queequeg in the practice of religious rites that Ishmael cannot understand. It so happens that the two men have to share a room and to sleep in the same bed.

Upon waking next morning about daylight, I found Queequeg's arm thrown over me in the most loving and affectionate manner. You had almost thought I had been his wife. The counterpane was of patchwork, full of odd little parti-coloured squares and triangles; and this arm of his tattooed all over with an interminable Cretan labyrinth of a figure ... looked for all the world like a strip of the same patchwork quilt.

[MELVILLE, 1851: 37]

Ishmael's half-thought that he might be married to Queequeg is one that any child might have of a father or brother. In the phantasy life of the unconscious, the identity of family members forms and un-forms under the aegis of the ancestor, as though they were the monads of time and space over which the One presides. There is an otherness to which the child in every adult cannot have access. Ishmael's perception of Queequeg is one that every son will know: the attempt to define a father is like the attempt to solve a mystery, and it cannot have a successful outcome. All intimate relationships are founded on an unknowable that has to be acknowledged if intimacy is to be sustained. Ishmael cannot comprehend the meaning of Queequeg's rites or of the tattoos on his skin. (In a remarkable piece of symbolism, the empty coffin that saves Ishmael from drowning was made by Queequeg.) And yet in this narrative the idea of a father is an aspiration rather than a realisation: there is no real father, and all potential fathers turn out to be at best brotherly. Ishmael's realisation that he might be married to Queequeg is passed over in a matter-of-fact way, as Ishmael's mind slides into a consideration of the cryptic patterning on the counterpane and the "interminable Cretan labyrinth" that he thinks to perceive in Queequeg's tattoos. A certain forming of the symbol appears to have collapsed, as in a return to the incoherence that characterised the painting in the building known as the Spouter-Inn. And yet the orbit of symbol formation is never lost.

> Like ethnic myths and legends of origins all over the world, the story of Abraham, Isaac and Jacob is an ethnogenesis designed to sustain the identity and destiny of the ethnic group within which it came into existence. As with the myths and legends of origins of other peoples, questions of historical accuracy are of secondary importance.
>
> [BLENKINSOPP, 2015: 166]

Ishmael, the pseudonym of the schoolmaster narrator of Melville's tale, never reveals his actual name. The use of a pseudonym has more than one meaning. It refers to a figure in the Bible, and in turn this reference is a reference to a certain type of place. Within these two references is an implication never consciously acknowledged: that any depth in meaning to name or place is brought about by the sacrifice, which in Platonic terms is the point of transition out of which the manifold forms from the One. The sacrifice renders a place sacred (this is what the word sacred means). It endows the place with a sense of awe and horror and spiritual turbulence, which again is what the sacred means. This is where God erupts. God in this case is the primordial ancestor, the author and victim of the sacrifice.

By his name, Melville's Ishmael lays claim to a spiritual affinity with Abraham's first-born son Ishmael, who was the son of an Egyptian mother, Hagar, and stigmatised as illegitimate. Cast in the role of outcast, Abraham's Ishmael finds his natural home in the wilderness. On the orders of his father, he is abandoned to the desert on two occasions. Divine grace alone saves him from death by dehydration. *Within this landscape of the spirit, the potential of the sacrifice defines the meaning of place and name.* The desert as a place of sacrifice decisively leaves its mark on an abandoned child. It forms his identity as a nomad and as a founding figure among the Bedouin. Melville's Ishmael is drawn to wilderness as the ocean rather than as the desert. Unlike Abraham's Ishmael, he is without lineage and he is no founder of a lineage. His one claim on the future is as the narrator of Melville's tale. His state of being spiritually a foundling is reflected in the state of nearly everyone he meets. The crew on board the *Pequod* and on other ships are like orphans in an institution.

The family is a prototype for the settled community that arises out of the wilderness of the desert. Theophany, as the power that inhabits the desert, determines that relationships within the family will be never straightforward. Under its forming idea, assertions of legitimacy and of illegitimacy, or acts of rejection, will take place within the grave lineaments of the family. The threat of the sacrifice, of the goat driven into the wilderness, hangs over both of Abraham's sons. Both of them are saved from death – one from dehydration and the other from a father's knife – by an act of grace. In either case the redemptive nature of theophany could not be more unlike the cataclysm of the white whale.

Theophany, and not good sense, determines succession. Abraham's family, generation upon generation, makes its hesitant way down the tunnel of spiritual darkness. Theophany is the one and only intermittent means of illumination. Abraham's grandson, Jacob, wrestles throughout the night by the Jabbok River with a figure who may or may not be an angel. Eventually this figure, in winning the fight, renames Jacob as Israel, or "the one who struggles with God". The incident establishes Jacob–Israel as the founder of the Israelites. But this claim depends on an unusual condition in order that it might be implemented: there has to be a back-formation of two generations to Abraham, who may indeed never have existed as other than an imaginary way of endorsing Jacob's claim. As time and space emerge from the One, they have the form of a past that informs the present moment, so that the present moment is able to validate the authority of the individual. In itself, the present moment is insufficient as a ground to carry the weight of revelation. Jacob's no doubt shocked realisation that he and Israel are one enables him retrospectively to bring completeness to the narrative of Abraham's life. Without insight into the miraculous recurrence that he has inherited, Jacob would have been unable to bear the responsibility of becoming Israel. I would characterise the struggle by the river, like Jacob's dream of the gate to heaven at Bethel, as having the significance of a sacrifice that endows an individual name and a place with the sacral meaning out of which a family might form.

History as it begins to take shape invokes the past as an

ancestral presence. It endorses any claim to spiritual insight that the present moment might wish to assert. Someone who moves like a sleepwalker within an ontology of the divine will have one hunger alone, which is for the theophanic. The sleepwalker in each of us moves in a certain direction. Our ancestors, through ages too obscure to be recalled, were similar sleepwalkers who walked within the compass of the divine. On this point, a history of unconscious reminiscence merges with an ontology of the sacred and loses any basis that it might have had in the historical event. The Platonic vision that would draw the manifold out of the One is no different. The primordial and mysterious figure from the past that defines the present fortunes of the family personifies the potency of the One in its relation to the manifold members of the family. I would define a figure of this kind as the progenitor. In the intuitions of silence, the veiled presence of the progenitor – as a version of the One – conveys the impression of an ancestor drawn from the immeasurable spaces of the wilderness.[2] If I should reverse the perspectives of time, I would find one generation as returning in thought to an earlier generation, under the influence of an actual or imaginary figure that is situated remotely and even without focus in the past or in the quite recent present. Ferdinand in *The Tempest* is inspired to fall in love when Ariel sings to him about the body of his dead father sunk in the ocean, full fathoms five.

[2] In a collection of very old family photographs, I find one photograph of a figure about whom I have no knowledge. Did this figure exist, and did it have a history? Or has this photograph in the family collection appeared in some fashion beyond my understanding? I have the fanciful thought that the mythic ancestor who determines our wayward lives is synonymous with Melville's white whale. This would give Ahab an impersonal motive in wishing to destroy it.

Ferdinand's actual father is still alive; the figure in the water is a figment of the imagination and yet a progenitor more real than any actual person in releasing Ferdinand's emotionality. The wilderness that forms the symbol in this case is the ocean rather than the desert. The effect of the imaginary body in the water, like the entry of silence into the mind, enables the immeasurable to command utterance. In the case of Ferdinand, it frees his ability to love. The wilderness, as the interim where the symbol forms, carries the death and rebirth of the sacrifice within it. The theophany that forms through ancestral vastness is without a past or future, as the immeasurable manifests itself through a landscape of silence.

Ontologies of the divine will precipitate madness if they should present themselves as unique. They require repetition, like the repeated enactment of the rite, as a means of insulation against dread. The unique in itself is unsafe; it cannot protect against the dead, which is the sacrifice when uncontained by rite. The fate of Melville's Pip, the black cabin boy, whose role in Melville's story is similar to the role played by the Fool in *King Lear*, is to suffer the unique.

> By the merest chance the ship itself at last rescued him; but from that hour the little black boy went about the deck as an idiot; such, they said he was. The sea had jeeringly thrown up his finite body, but drowned the infinite of his soul. Not drowned entirely, though. Rather carried it down alive to wondrous depths, where strange shapes of the un-warped primal world glided to and fro before his passive eyes. . . . He saw God's foot upon the treadle of the loom, and spoke of

it; and therefore his shipmates called him mad.

[MELVILLE, 1851: 355]

Pip's vision is complete; it is not cryptic; and it puts him beyond the pale. To enter the theophanic dimension is to be committed to the in-between state that lies between the One and the manifold, which is the wilderness. The notions of lineage and inheritance in Genesis are ways in which the godhead manifests itself through the idea of the family. Moses is an exception. His fate in entering the darkness is unique. He belongs to the family of Abraham and yet in the condition that he is like the outcast nomad of Melville's story. He is unattached by birth and marriage to any one tribe. It requires the theophany of the burning bush to transform him into an inspired leader. The Israelites, claims Shemaryahu Talmon, saw the desert as "a cursed wasteland that had to be traversed, . . . as a frightening and unwelcome phenomenon" that was no more than "a bridge to communal salvation in history" and that "only with Christianity was it raised from the status of a temporary disengagement to that of a theological ideal" (Talmon, 1966: 63). And yet for the Israelites the wilderness was the necessary ground for a revelation that took the form of falling manna, of unfamiliar clouds of redemption, and of a voice that names itself enigmatically.

The wilderness can be hauntingly beautiful, even as it brings the traveller within the orbit of death. It is the place where the sacrifice takes place, outside the city wall, beyond the reach of human law. Its conjunction with the desert or ocean is not coincidental. Apparitions arise at the point at which a Platonic notion of time and space form. These apparitions are not hallucinations. They are intuitions of a metaphysical reality.

Two narratives appear seemingly out of nowhere (the text of Genesis or the writings of Melville). Certain obvious markers, like the linking of a name, turn out to be dead as metaphors, in spite of a phantom after-effect. Absences in one text correlate with presences in another text, like congruent dreams that side by side throw light on each other. Genesis and Melville's novel are absences that in haunting each other turn out to be semblances of a concurring presence. The one centre is the whirling powers of the theophany. Between the forming of the symbol and the informing of time and space as a conception of a past there can be no calculation, since time is still in the process of being formed out of the unfathomable. This is the significance of the wilderness. For the Platonist, the immeasurable is able to release the numinous manifold and to transform any object within its gaze. The shaping of art lies in this affirmation. Transfused by the strange, the object is overwhelming in its impression of otherness.[3] The truth of our statements and of our behaviour is validated by the extent to which the radiance of the One falls upon them.

> Imagine a sheer, steep crag, of reddish appearance below, extending into eternity; on top there is this ridge, which looks down over a projecting rim into a bottomless chasm. Now imagine what a person would

[3] Bruegel's fascination with the subject of the Tower of Babel is the fascination of someone who discovers the symbol in silence. His fascination overrides the less-than-clear claim in Genesis that a divine disapproval of the building of the tower resulted in a confusion of tongues.

probably experience if he put his foot on the edge of
the ridge which overlooks the chasm and found no
solid footing and nothing to hold onto. . . . *The time
to keep silent* (Eccles. 3: 7) is when reason touches on
those things which are beyond it.

[GREGORY OF NYSSA, *THE ABYSS OF KNOWLEDGE* (COMMENTARY ON
ECCLESIASTES, SERMON 7, IN DANIÉLOU, 1962]

The entry of silence into the active life marks a breakdown. It
is like the death of a stranger during a convivial moment. In
the contemplative life, the relation of silence and death entails
abandoning all positions in a more resigned fashion. "In the
soul an 'uncreated something' . . . is an alien land and wilderness. It is more unnamed than possessing a name, and more
unknown than it is known. If you could annihilate yourself
in an instant (or rather quicker than an instant) you would be
everything that it is in itself" (Eckhart, in McGinn, 1994: 170).

Mind in terms of the active life shows itself to be a
repository for memory and anticipation. In Socrates' theory
of recollection, all knowledge is latent in mind and waits to be
released. The ontology of the *Timaeus*, in which a demiurge
extracts time and space from an immeasurable One, is compat-
ible with the theory of recollection when, and only when, it is
seen to describe a transformation in the mental depths rather
than a cosmology "out there". The One as the ground to all
meaning enables mind to be meaningful through a release of
the manifold in the form of time and space. In effect time and
space form out of the One as symbols.

The notion of climbing a ladder that eventually has to
be discarded is Wittgenstein's metaphoric way of thinking

114

about the approach in his *Tractatus* to the final assertion that "whereof one cannot speak, thereof one must be silent" (Wittgenstein, 1922: 189). The metaphor links silence on a spiritual level to the active life. It voids silence of any other meaning than to be an absence of speech or of sound in general. The climber makes no allowance for the contemplative belief that the immeasurable is an active potency, rather than a vague and distanced promise. For the magnitude of the immeasurable within silence is such that it can disorder all tongues (and this would be a way of thinking about Wittgenstein's assertion). In the active life I say: whereof one cannot speak, thereof one must be silent. In the contemplative life I say: whereof one must be silent, thereof one cannot speak.[4] This is to know the sacred. ("Whereof one must be silent" sounds like the name of a god.) Silence disables all means of communication, or it renders them numinous. It is a modality that takes mind out of this world.

Coleridge and Lossky, each in his own way, sees a means of communication between the increate and the created world. The disabling element in the message is one that they

[4] Paul Wienpahl (1958) has compared Wittgenstein's ladder to the Buddha's understanding of the limited usefulness of a raft. "While the Tathagata, in his teachings, constantly makes use of conceptions and ideas about them, disciples should keep in mind the unreality of such conceptions and ideas. They should recall that the Tathagata, in making use of them in explaining the Dharma always uses them in the resemblance of a raft that is of use only to cross a river. As the raft is of no further use after the river is crossed, it should be discarded. So these arbitrary conceptions of things and about things should be wholly given up as one attains enlightenment" (*The Diamond Sutra*). Wittgenstein believes that while the beauty in logic, language and natural law can be gestured forth, it cannot be explained. "Language cannot represent that which mirrors itself in language" (*Tractatus* 4.121). "What can be shown cannot be said" (*Tractatus* 4.1212). "It used to be said that God could create anything except that which was contrary to the laws of logic. The truth is, we could not say how an 'un-logical' world would look" (*Tractatus* 3.031).

do not touch on. They do not touch on the meaning of a potential breakdown in the means of communication. The influence of the past and future on the present moment is without meaning in the life of silence. What is there before me, vibrant in perception, is an emanation whose relation, if any, to the linear or to any other means of discrimination is obscure. This is the point of my book: the immeasurable arrived at through an experience of silence shows itself not to be a wan or abstracted concept. It shows itself to be an immeasurable potency that forces me to turn about the direction from which I began. It is not the act of opening the mind to silence that initiates the coming into being of the symbol; it is the immeasurable discovered through this act and at first underrated that performs this act.

The active life presumes history to be a preconception in mind. It thinks of succession as meaningful in itself. The contemplative life assumes that mind depends on a different preconception, in which ontology is founded in certain assumptions of a triadic nature. In Platonism the triadic nature has the form of the One in its relation to time and space. In Christian belief it is the Father in relation to the Holy Spirit and to the Son. The active life immerses itself in the values of experience. It postulates that experience is the centre to being. The past and the future, as meaningful adjuncts to the present, are like points of departure or arrival on the railway line that is history. The contemplative life has its centre elsewhere. It moves by way of silence towards the immeasurable. The one experience that it values is its means of entry into the non-experiential. In silence the time and space of Platonic inspiration renounce identity and return into the One.

If I centre myself on the values of experience, I may set dream aside as mumbo-jumbo, as the empiricist John Locke did, or I may think of it as meaningful according to the prescription that dream is meaningful, in so far as it can be centred on experience. But dream resists this way of thinking; it pulls away from the claim to centrality that experience can imply. Dream in relation to experience will always appear to be a strange rubric. In the contemplative life, the understanding of dream as code has no meaning. Dreams evacuate mind from the thrall of experience, so that (as in Plato's *Phaedrus*) the dreamer, when freed from the dream, is able to ascend towards the immeasurable.

Plato's demiurge, in personifying intelligence, dis-unites or forms the manifolds that constitute the world. The immeasurable as the One is the ground to transformation. At the point of transformation is the wilderness. The symbol, as it settles in the world, accommodates itself to a place that no map has described. It is inimical to the discipline of history. What I think of as without me is also within me. The fact that I exist is a subject for awe. I cannot believe it. And yet I exist. It is as though existence itself were perceived through the perspective of a reversed telescope. At the point at which the manifold emerges out of the One, or at which it returns to it, silence and history cross paths as they go on their separate ways.

A letter from Joshua Durban

Joshua came to dinner. I told him how the title *Silence & the Disorder of Tongues* had come to me without my understanding how silence might be related to a disorder of tongues. Astonished, he told Maria and myself the story of how, deep in the night while attempting to sleep in a Korean monastery high in the mountains, the intensity of the silence appeared to force its way into his mouth and broke apart any attempt at speech. I began to understand how on this occasion silence and the disorder of tongues might be related. Here is his letter.

It seems so long ago since you first told me about your book. I remember how amazed I was by the subject. I immediately felt the need to share with you and Maria some of my experiences in the Korean mountains, while staying at my monastery. It was very early on in my training as a monk that I came to realize the interwoven, elusive presences of noise and silence and the myriad ways in which they might upset the balance of our so-called rational minds. It became apparent on the first day I arrived at the monastery, climbing fiercely and full of determination the steep mountain road leading to it. Since it was winter-time and sunset was approaching I was loath to spend the night in the woods. I hurried along, only to be greeted by a closed wooden gate. Following the customary well-behaved-monk's etiquette I sat silently and waited for the gate to open. It took a very long time indeed. It became dark. As I sat there freezing, trying to meditate, I realized how much noise my mind had created while climbing up: the desire to get there, to escape fear, to meet my fellow monks, to eat, to have a nice warm cup of green tea, to prove how eager and serious I was, to soak in a hot bath, to sleep. The sudden contrast of just sitting there, waiting, not knowing when the gates will open, made my inner turmoil all the more present. And the silence which it encountered all the more menacing. The silence of absence. Of something impenetrable and non-responsive.

The gates finally creaked open and the head monk came out to greet me. "Did you climb?" he asked. "Yes" I answered eagerly "very quickly". " But did you climb?" He asked patiently, smiling gently. Silence. Confused, somewhat disorganized I was at a loss for words. "Why don't you go down then" he suggested, "and climb?" "Again" I gasped. Silence. The gates closed.

I descended into the darkness. The woods were full of night noises: the arctic wind, night-creatures and the loud beatings of my heart. I slept fitfully and in the break of dawn started climbing up. Again? This time, a strange silence enveloped me. I was walking very slowly, mindfully, savouring each step, each tree, each fleeting cloud, every dew-drop and each snow-covered flower. The world became utterly silent, time disappeared. I was suddenly inside the monastery, sipping tea. Where was I when I was climbing?

After a long and busy day of working, training, meditating and getting used to the hustle and bustle of monastic life (so different from the serene, quiet image we idealize in the West) I finally went to sleep. Lying in my room on the heated wooden floor, safely tucked under the warm blanket, with an open window framing the snow-fall and the surrounding mountains shrouded in mist, it grew darker and darker. And silent. At first a dreadful silence. It was palpable, tangible, pulsating. Silence became an object. A terrifying object. The contrast between the warmth of feeling contained and content, the well-being of my fetus-like position and the dreadful disappearance of daytime noise was almost unbearable. My internal cacophony became very loud the more I encountered this omnipresent silent object. It reflected my lack of internal quiet while, at the same time, threatened me with annihilation. I think it was as near as I ever got to experiencing death while still being alive. I tried to speak, to call out to someone. But the silence was so intense, so physical, that I felt it was entering my mouth, breaking up any attempt I made to articulate speech. I was thrown back to sensory-memory from my childhood, where sometimes, at night, I would feel so smothered by silence that my tongue grew heavy and I was not even able to cry out.

After a while, however, the fear subsided. The warmth of the comforting floor and blanket blended with the outside snow and mountains and a different kind of silence, a quietness permeated me. This feeling of transcending quietude, of true silence, brought about a tremendous feeling of bliss. Since everything was one, it was empty. This quiet-silence-emptiness could only appear, I think, after my unbearable encounter with internal noise, the crumbling down of the defensive ego followed by a severely disorganized state and the ensuing willingness to just be there. Not doing a thing. One and everyone.

I hope to see you and Maria soon.
Affectionately,
Joshua (JiDam Do-Ban)

nstrong, A. H. (Trans. & Ed.) (1967). *Plotinus: Ennead III*. Cambridge, MA: Harvard University Press.

ton J. (1991). *Understanding the Fourth Gospel*. Oxford: Clarendon Press.

in, I. (1996). *The Sense of Reality*. London: Chatto & Windus.

:kman, A. M. (1916). The Pharaoh's Placenta and the Moon-God Khons. *Journal of Egyptian Archeology, III*.

ikinsopp, J. (2011). *Creation, Un-creation, Re-creation*. London: T&T Clark International.

ikinsopp, J. (2015). *Abraham: The Story of a Life*. Grand Rapids, MI: Eerdmans.

wn, R. E. (1966). *The Gospel According to John (i–xii)*. London: Geoffrey Chapman, 1971.

ur, B. G. (2008). Foreordained from all eternity: The mystery of the Incarnation according to some early Christian and Byzantine writers. *Dumbarton Oak Papers, 62*.

tmann, R. (1964). *The Gospel of John: A Commentary*, trans. G. R. Beasley-Murray, R. W. N. Hoare, & J. K. Riches. Oxford: Blackwell, 1971.

ment, O. 1985. *Orient-Occident. Deux passeurs: Vladimir Lossky et Paul Evdokimov*. Geneva: Éditions Labor et Fides.

ourn, K. (Ed.) (1961). *The Notebooks of Samuel Taylor Coleridge, Vol. 2: 1804–1809*. Princeton, NJ: Princeton University Press, 1980.

eridge, S. T. (1817a). *Biographia Literaria*, ed. J. Engell & W. Jackson Bate. Princeton, NJ: Princeton University Press, 1983.

eridge, S. T. (1817b). *Biographia Literaria*, ed. G. Watson. London: Dent, 1965.

ledge, E., & McGinn, B. (Eds. & Trans.) (1981). *Meister Eckhart: The Essential Sermons, Commentaries, Treatises and Defense*. Mahwah, NJ: Paulist Press.

bin, H. (1954). Avicenna and the Visionary Recital, trans. W. R. Trask. Princeton, NJ: Princeton University Press, 1960.

bin, H. (1973). The theme of the voyage and the messenger. In: *The Voyage and the Messenger: Iran and Philosophy*, trans. J. Rowe. Berkeley, CA: North Atlantic Books, 1998.

tingham, J., Stoothoff, R., & Murdoch, D. (1984). *The Philosophical Writings of Descartes, Vol. 2*. Cambridge: Cambridge University Press.

iélou, J. (1962). *From Glory to Glory*, trans. H. Musurillo. London: John Murray.

aux, A. A., & de Lussy, F. (Eds.) (1997). *Simone Weil Oeuvres Completes, Tome 6 (Vol. 2: Septembre 1941–Février 1942)*. Paris: Éditions Gallimard

dd, C. H. (1953). *The Interpretation of the Fourth Gospel*. Cambridge: Cambridge University Press.

dds, E. R. (1960). Tradition and personal achievement in the philosophy of Plotinus. *The Journal of Roman Studies, 50*.

Edwards, M. (1991). Middle Platonism on the beautiful and the good. *Mnemosyne, 44* (1–2).

Eliade, M. (1949). *The Myth of the Eternal Return.* New York: Princeton Pantheon, 19!

Eliot, T. S. (1936). *Burnt Norton.* In: *Four Quartets.* London: Faber & Faber, 1944.

Emmet, D. (1966). Theoria and the way of life. *The Journal of Theological Studies, 17.*

Gerson, L. P. (Trans. & Ed.) (2013). *Plotinus: Ennead V.5. That the Intelligibles are not external to the Intellect, and on the Good.* Las Vegas, CA: Parmenides.

Griffin, E. (Ed.) (1981). *The Cloud of Unknowing.* New York: Harper Collins.

Hägg, H. F. (2006). *Clement of Alexandria and the Beginning of Christian Apophaticism* Oxford: Oxford: University Press.

Harland, J. P. (1998). Vertical or horizontal: The sin of Babel. *Vetus Testamentum, 48* (515–533.

Heschel, A. (1962). *The Prophets.* New York: HarperCollins, 2001.

Hiebert, T. (1996). *The Yahwist's Landscape: Nature and Religion in Early Israel.* Minneapolis, MN: Fortress Press.

Jarczyk G. & Labattière P-J. 1995. *Maître Eckhart ou l'empreinte du desert.* Paris: Albin Michel.

Kahn, C. H. (1979). *The Art and Thought of Heraclitus.* Cambridge: Cambridge University Press.

Kavanaugh, K., & Rodriguez, O. (Trans.) (1966). *The Collected Works of St John of the Cross.* London: Thomas Nelson, 1991.

Kuper, H. (1947). *An African Aristocracy: Rank among the Swazi.* New York: Africana Publishing House, 1980.

Lau, D. C. (Trans.) (1963). *Lao Tzu: Tao Te Ching.* Harmondsworth: Penguin.

Lee, D. (Trans.) (1965). *Plato: Timaeus and Critias.* Harmondsworth: Penguin.

Lossky, V. (1944). *The Mystical Theology of the Eastern Church.* Crestwood, NY: St Vladimir's Seminary Press, 1957.

Lossky, V. (1949). Panagia. In: *In the Image and Likeness of God* (pp. 195–210). Crestwood, NY: St Vladimir's Seminary Press, 1974.

Lossky, V. (1959). Traditions and tradition. In: *In the Image and Likeness of God.* (pp. 141–168). Crestwood, NY: St Vladimir's Seminary Press, 1974

Lossky, V. (1978). *Orthodox Theology*, trans. I. Kesarcodi-Watson & I. Kesarcodi-Wats Crestwood, NY: St Vladimir's Seminary Press.

Luibheid, C. (Trans.) (1987). *Pseudo-Dionysius: The Complete Works.* New York: Paulis Press.

Malamoud, C. (1989). *Cooking the World: Ritual and Thought in Ancient India*, trans. White. Delhi: Oxford University Press, 1996.

Malherbe, A. J., & Ferguson, E. (1978). *Gregory of Nyssa: The Life of Moses.* New York:

Paulist Press.

uss, M. (1926). Critique interne de la "legende d'Abraham". In: *Marcel Mauss, Oeuvres 2: Représentations collectives et diversité des civilisations*, ed. V. Karady. Paris: Éditions de Minuit, 1974.

Ginn, B. (1981). The God beyond God: Theology and mysticism in the thought of Meister Eckhart. *The Journal of Religion, 61* (2).

Ginn, B. (1994). Ocean and sea as symbols of mystical absorption in the Christian tradition. *The Journal of Religion, 74* (2).

Ginn, B. (2001). *The Mystical Thought of Meister Eckhart.* New York: Crossroad Publishing.

Keever, I. (2015). Painting on the threshold. *Royal Academy of Arts Magazine, 126.*

lville, H. (1851). *Moby Dick: or, The White Whale.* London: Collins, 1953.

yendorff, J. (1987). Wisdom–Sophia: Contrasting approaches to a complex theme. *Dumbarton Oak Papers, 41.*

chell, S. (Trans.) (1984). *Rainer Maria Rilke: Letters to a Young Poet.* New York: Random House.

nk, R. (1990). *Ludwig Wittgenstein: The Duty of Genius.* London: Vintage, 1991.

las, P. (1987). *Deification in Christ: Orthodox Perspectives on the Nature of the Human Person*, trans. N. Russell. Crestwood, NY: St Vladimir's Seminary.

cal, B. (1670). *Pensées de Pascal*, ed. P. Sellier. Paris: Bordas, 1991.

ley, M. (Trans.) (1973). *Franz Kafka: Shorter Works, Vol. 1.* London: Secker & Warburg.

pp, W. H. C. (1999). *Exodus 1–18.* New York: Doubleday.

pp, W. H. C. (2006). *Exodus 19–40.* New York: Doubleday.

ch, H.-C. (1938). La Ténèbre mystique chez le Pseudo-Denys l'Aréopagite. In: *En quête de la Gnose, Tome 1.* Paris: Gallimard, 1978.

ndel Harris, J. (1917). *The Origin of the Prologue to St John's Gospel.* Cambridge: Cambridge University Press.

nou, L. (1949). Le valeur du silence dans la culte védique. *Journal of the American Oriental Society, 69* (1).

nou, L., & Filliozat, J. (1953). *L'Inde classique, Vol. 2.* Paris: Maisonneuve; Paris: École Française d'Extrême-Orient, 2001.

nou, L., & Silburn, L. (1949). Sur la notion du Bráhman. *Journal Asiatique, 237*: 7–46.

ssell, B. (1925). *The ABC of Relativity.* Abingdon: Routledge, 2009.

e, G. (1951) (with A. C. Lloyd & I. Murdoch). Thinking and language. *Proceedings of the Aristotelian Society, 25*: 65–82. [Suppl.: Freedom, Language and Reality]

pp, E., & Hutchison, P. (Trans. & Eds.) (1998). *Johann Wolfgang von Goethe: Maxims and Reflections.* London: Penguin.

Talmon, S. (1966). The "Desert Motif" in the Bible and in Qumran literature. In: *Bibli Motifs: Origins and Transformations*, ed. A. Altmann. Cambridge, MA: Harvard University Press.

Von Rad, G. (1970). *Wisdom in Israel*. London: SCM Press, 1972.

Watson, B. (1993). Introduction. In: *Lao Tzu: Tao Te Ching*, trans. S. Addiss & S. Lombardo. Boston, MA, & London: Shambala, 2007.

Wensinck, A. J. (Trans.) (1923). *Mystical Treatises of Isaac of Nineveh*. Amsterdam: Uttgave der Koninklijke Akademie van Wetenschappen.

Wienpahl, P. (1958). Zen and the work of Wittgenstein. *Chicago Review, 12* (2): 67–72

Wijngaards, J. N. M. (1975). The awe-inspiring reality of Christ's silence. *Indian Journ of Theology, 24*.

Williams, G. H. (1962). *Wilderness and Paradise in Christian Thought*. New York: Har

Wittgenstein, L. (1922). *Tractatus Logico-Philosophicus*. London: Routledge & Kegan Paul.

Wittgenstein, L. (1967). *Remarks on Frazer's "Golden Bough"*. Doncaster: Brynmill Pre 1979.

Without movement you climb the mountain.
Oh intellect!
The path leads you
To a wonderful desert,
So large, so distant
Without extent
No place, no time
Unique
It is the Good.
No foot leaves a trace
Created meaning
Has never gone there
There it is. No one knows why
It is here, it is there
It is far, it is near
It is deep, it is high
This is how it is
Neither here nor there.

(From *Granum Synapsis* or T*he Mustard Seed*,
a poem attributed to Meister Eckhart.
In Jarczyk & Labarrière 1995: 12-13)

Acknowledgements.

My thanks to Maria, Judith, Martin, Paul and the other friends who have helped to improve the text.